THE WRECK OF THE *Sv. NIKOLAI*

THE
WRECK
OF THE
Sv. NIKOLAI

TWO NARRATIVES OF THE FIRST RUSSIAN EXPEDITION
to the
OREGON COUNTRY
1808-1810

Edited with an Introduction by
KENNETH N. OWENS

Translation by
ALTON S. DONNELLY

WESTERN IMPRINTS

The Press of the Oregon Historical Society

1985

Frontis: The Wreck of the *Sv. Nikolai* (1 November 1808)

Support for the production of this volume in part by the Westland Foundation.

This volume was designed and produced by Western Imprints, The Press of the Oregon Historical Society.

The paper used in this publication meets the minimum requirements of American National Standard for Information Sciences—Permanence of Paper for Printed Library Materials, ANSI Z39.48-1984.

Library of Congress Cataloging in Publication Data

The Wreck of Sv. Nikolai

   (North Pacific studies; no. 8)
   First work, translation of: Krushenie Rossiĭsko-amerikanskoĭ kompanii sudna "Sviatoĭ Nikolaĭ," pod nachálstvom shturmana Bulygina, pri severo-zapadnykh beregakh Ameriki.
   Subtitle: The narrative of Timofei Tarakanov, translated from the 1874 Russian edition, and the narrative of Ben Hobucket, a Quileute oral tradition.
   Includes index.
   1. Oregon—Description and travel. 2. Oregon—History—To 1859. 3. Russians—Oregon—History—19th century. 4. Quileute Indians—First contact with Occidental civilization. 5. Indians of North America—Oregon—First contact with Occidental civilization. 6. Tarakanov, Timofeĭ. I. Owens, Kenneth N. II. Tarakanov, Timofeĭ. Krushenie Rossiĭsko-amerikanskoĭ kompanii sudna "Sviatoĭ Nikolaĭ," pod nachal stvom shturmana Bulygina, pri severo-zapadnykh beregakh Ameriki. English. 1984. III. Hobucket, Ben. First coming of the White people to Quileute. 1984. IV. Title. V. Series.
F880.W96 1984   979.5'02   83-15138
ISBN 0-87595-124-4   (Alk. paper)

Printed in the United States of America.

North Pacific Studies Series

Contents

Illustrations

Preface

At its beginning, this work seemed to us a project of rare simplicity. We meant to translate for publication, with a short introduction and sparse annotation, a document unique in the frontier history of colonial North America, Timofei Tarakanov's narrative of the wreck of the *Sv. Nikolai*. Then our simple project became steadily more complex. We discovered a parallel account preserved in the Quileute oral tradition, Ben Hobucket's narrative, a source that certainly should be published alongside the Tarakanov story. More perplexing, we encountered a problem regarding Tarakanov's identity that led us into a long-standing controversy regarding Ivan Petrov, Hubert Howe Bancroft's Russian translator and researcher. The result was a lengthy investigation, with conclusions that are set forth in the appendix to this volume. Along the way we found it necessary to deal with such issues as the paternity of a remarkable Makah person, Tarakanov's benefactor, and the literary career of Albert Reagan, Hobucket's rather unusual scribe. All matters raised research problems that needed attention before we could bring our task to an end.

Some of these issues came to have a compelling interest, even as they absorbed far more time than we first intended to give to the project. As our investigations continued, we concluded that Tarakanov's adventure should not be depicted merely as an incidental episode in the early history of the Oregon Country. If placed within its international context, the *Sv. Nikolai*'s 1808 voyage has a significance for Russia's expansion in North America that might be compared, for example, to the 1540 expedition of Francisco Vásquez de Coronado on the northern borderlands frontier of New Spain. Considered together, the Tarakanov account and the Hobucket tradition can also contribute to a reevaluation of native relations with Europeans during the era of the sea otter trade. For anyone whose expectations either of the Russians or of the native peoples have been molded by popular stereotypes, there are surprises to be found in these documents.

As our work on the project expanded, we were fortunate to find many others who shared our interest, answered our inquiries, and gave us assistance on research problems. Often we received the benefit as well of an informed skepticism, prompting a more rigorous examination of the evidence. Our debt of gratitude extends through a wide network of scholarly acquaintances, professional associates, and friends in the United States, Canada, and the USSR. Unfailingly, we have met with a spirit of scholarly cooperation and generosity that exceeded every expectation.

Among particular acknowledgments we would like to thank the staff at The Bancroft Library, that great research institution at the University of California, Berkeley, and especially Marie Burn and Irene Moran. They proved willing collaborators, even while we were engaged in demonstrating that certain of The Bancroft's documents were not what they have been purported to be. The collaboration involved also a trio of interlibrary loan experts: Kathryn King of California State University, Sacramento; Jo Lynn Milardovich, now at the University of California, Berkeley; and Vera Troitsky of the Bartell Library at the State University of New York, Binghamton. Their skills and their willingness to search out difficult items have been extraordinary. To them and to their institutions we are grateful.

A number of individuals and repositories have located rare publications or important documents for us, and in some cases supplied us with copies. For their assistance we would like to thank: Hollis Scott, University Archivist, Harold B. Lee Library, Brigham Young University; Mary S. Pratt, History Department, Los Angeles Public Library; Jean R. McNiece, Manuscripts and Archives Division, The New York Public Library; and the directors and staffs of the Library of Congress, Washington, D.C., the

Beinecke Library, Yale University, New Haven, and the Lenin Library in Moscow.

Problems of evidence and issues of interpretation led us to call upon specialists in many different areas. Gerald E. Grosso, formerly curator for the Ozette Archaeological Project, Neah Bay, Washington, helped with matters of Makah and Quileute nomenclature. E. A. P. Crownhart-Vaughan of the Oregon Historical Society offered important suggestions on questions of Russian terminology for trade goods. Antoinette Shalkop very graciously volunteered her expertise to supply information from the Alaska Russian Orthodox Church Collection in the Library of Congress, while her evidence and opinions enhanced our understanding of Ivan Petrov. For her assistance in resolving a number of obscure points we wish to express our warm appreciation to Svetlana G. Fedorova of the Institute of Ethnography in the Academy of Sciences of the USSR, Moscow. Richard A. Pierce of Queen's University, Kingston, Ontario, was extremely generous in sharing his knowledge of Russian sources and manuscript collections, especially the Russian American Company documents in the National Archives, Washington, D.C. Finally, special thanks are due to Morgan B. Sherwood of the University of California, Davis. The scholar who first broached the Ivan Petrov issue in print, Professor Sherwood aided us with his encouragement and with detailed coaching about the problems and perils of Petrov historiography.

Finally, we would like to acknowledge our appreciation for the efforts of Bruce Taylor Hamilton, executive editor, and the skilled staff at Western Imprints, The Press of the Oregon Historical Society, for their care in editing and rechecking details, in addition to their expertise in design and production. We are pleased and honored to have our work included in Western Imprints' prestigious North Pacific Studies Series.

Kenneth N. Owens
Sacramento, California

Alton S. Donnelly
Binghamton, New York

Editorial Principles

A brief note on the style of translation and transliteration: throughout we use a modified version of the Library of Congress system of transliteration, with some few departures from an exact transliteration in favor of an established usage. Thus for ships' names, we give *Sv. Nikolai* rather than *St. Nicholas*, the *Kad'iak* rather than *Kodiak*, and *Il'men* rather than either *Il'mena* or *Lady*. A few Russian and native words that have become familiar in the historical literature, such as *promyshlennik* and *toyon*, we leave untranslated instead of supplying less precise terms like fur-hunter or chieftain. We also leave untranslated certain less familiar terms that have a special meaning, repeatedly used in the Tarakanov account: *Koliuzhi*, for example, and *starshina*. In all these cases we supply a translation in brackets [ ] after the word in its first appearance and in some instances a footnote explanation as well. At a few points we also bracket the Russian original for some special terms after our first translation, such as supercargo [*prikash-chik*] and savages [*dikari*].

We have retained most Russian units of measurement, with an equivalent English measurement indicated in brackets.

For the sake of consistency, we have modernized the spelling of Ivan Petrov and Vasilii Petrovich Tarakanov throughout, following The Bancroft Library's current practice, even though the man wrote his own name Ivan Petroff and spelled Vassili Petrovitch Tarakanoff as the name of his quasi-fictional character.

The Russian American colony at New Arkhangel

THE WRECK OF THE *Sv. NIKOLAI*

Introduction

Introduction

On 1 November 1808, the shipwreck of the Russian schooner *Sv. Nikolai* (*St. Nicholas*) began a remarkable episode in the history of the Oregon Country. The two original narratives published in this volume, here brought together for the first time, provide the major documentary record of this shipwreck and the events that ensued. The story they describe is, in many ways, more compelling than any fictional account. It is a tale of adventure with moments of superb drama, a touch of comedy, and eventually a sad, even tragic fate for the two romantic figures at its center. And these events have historical importance that give significance to the two narratives as evidence of Russian activity and native responses early in the course of the Pacific Northwest's development.

Even in brief outline the story has interest. The *Sv. Nikolai* was a small ship owned by the Russian American Company. At the end of September 1808, it sailed from the Alaskan port of New Arkhangel (modern Sitka) with a party of twenty-two, under the command of Navigator Nikolai Isaakovich Bulygin. The group included Navigator Bulygin's wife, Anna Petrovna, twelve Russians and one Englishman who were employees of the Company, and five men and two women identified as Kodiak Aleuts.[1]

Aleksandr Baranov, the crude and brilliant first chief manager of the Russian American Company, had organized this expedition as a voyage of reconnaissance. Bulygin and his shipmates were ordered to explore the coast south of Vancouver Island, barter with the natives for sea otter pelts, and if possible discover a site for a permanent Russian post in the Oregon Country. Although Baranov had earlier sent Russian and Aleut parties southward to hunt sea otter in the waters off Spanish California, the voyage of the *Sv. Nikolai* was his first move in an ambitious plan to build a permanent commercial empire linking Alaska with the Oregon and California coasts.[2]

Less than five weeks after the voyage began, the ship was becalmed, then driven ashore by heavy seas. The site was a sandy beach just north of James Island and the mouth of the Quillayute River, above the modern town of La Push, Washington, on the present Quileute Indian Reservation.

This volume's two narratives, one of Russian origin and the other derived from a Quileute oral tradition, record the circumstances of the shipwreck and the adventures of the Russian party when they sought safety ashore. After salvaging a part of their cargo, the Russians clashed with the Quileute people in whose territory they were transgressing. The expedition members soon abandoned most of their supplies and fled south, into the country of the Hoh people. There, a few days after the shipwreck, the natives used a clever ruse to capture two men and two of the women in the party, including Anna Petrovna Bulygin. The rest fled toward the interior and spent a miserable winter struggling to avoid starvation; they plundered native camps, occasionally fighting with small groups of natives, and vainly sought some way they might be rescued.

At length, as the Tarakanov narrative describes, the group moved back toward the coast, hoping they might escape the natives and make contact with a trading vessel. But then they discovered that Mrs. Bulygin was living with the Makah people, apparently comfortable and content. When they made plans to steal her back, she rejected the idea and urged instead that the Russians surrender to her captors. The principal leader among these people, she explained, was an eminent man, upright and virtuous, who would assist the Russian refugees aboard a trading ship so they might return to Alaska at the first opportunity. After intense debate, a few of the party did surrender and came to live with the Makah. The rest, as the Hobucket narrative ex-

4

plains, attempted a desperate escape by sea. But they too were all captured or forced to surrender, and most of these expedition members became captives or slaves among the Hoh and Quileute.

Finally, in the spring of 1810, a Yankee captain sailing for the Russian American Company put in along this coast and learned the fate of the *Sv. Nikolai*'s castaways. By paying an expensive ransom he rescued thirteen survivors of the original twenty-two and returned them to New Arkhangel. Another American shipmaster purchased one or two more expedition members from natives along the Columbia River. Nearly all the rest, including Navigator Bulygin and his wife Anna Petrovna, had meanwhile perished.

Chief Manager Baranov had to write off this expedition as a costly failure. Guided in part we may assume by the reports of the survivors, he abandoned all further efforts to establish a post in the Oregon Country, directing the Company's expansion instead to the California coast where his employees founded Ross Colony in 1812. The story of the *Sv. Nikolai* and its crew's adventures soon faded to obscurity, lost to historical memory except for brief mention in the authorized accounts of the Company's activities in America.

The two narratives of these events, which permit the episode to be reconstructed in detail, have unique histories of their own. The Russian narrative originates with Timofei Osipovich Tarakanov, the Company's supercargo on the voyage, who, immediately after his rescue and return to New Arkhangel, described his adventures to Navy Captain V. M. Golovnin. Captain Golovnin took great interest in Tarakanov's recital. A person of genuine literary and scholarly skills, Golovnin first verified certain matters of detail, then prepared the account for publication in Russia. In form, Golovnin's work presented a straightforward narrative of events, tinged only slightly by Tarakanov's efforts to justify his own controversial actions and by Golovnin's occasional touches of moralism.

The Quileute account comes from a less direct source, an oral historical tradition that was preserved among the Quileute people for about one hundred years. In the early part of the twentieth century Ben Hobucket, a Quileute folk historian, asked a local official of the federal Indian service to write down this tradition. The official, Albert Reagan, published his version of Hobucket's oral account some twenty-five years later, in 1934. As he recorded it, the Quileute tradition had a description of the shipwreck and the ensuing events from the natives' perspective. But Hobucket's story also incorporated an additional brief narrative of the experiences of one of the Russian party, an Aleut woman who had remained with the group attempting to escape by sea, but who then surrendered to the Quileute and lived with Ben Hobucket's family until she was traded to or ransomed by the Russians.

The Hobucket tradition, though shorter than the Tarakanov narrative, offers a parallel version that reinforces Tarakanov's story at point after point, adds further detail, and explains some events and clarifies some allusions left unclear by Tarakanov's statement.

The connection between these two sources has previously escaped the attention of historians. Russian scholars have made sporadic use of the Tarakanov narrative in Golovnin's edition; but in English it has appeared only in two incomplete summaries. The Hobucket account, meanwhile, has remained totally obscure. Ben Hobucket and Albert Reagan both believed that the tradition described the shipwreck of an early Spanish expedition in Quileute territory. Other authors interested in Northwest Coast ethnology also have referred to the account as a Spanish voyage, accepting the uninformed opinion of Reagan and Hobucket without learning more about European exploration along the shores of the Oregon Country. But a close comparison leaves no doubt that this source, so different in its origin, does indeed refer to the same events described by Tarakanov when he returned to New Arkhangel in 1810. These two narratives provide independent verification for the history of the 1808 *Sv. Nikolai* expedition.

The editing of these accounts, at first appearance a simple task, has proved to be a project with a full share of complications and a few genuine surprises. Each document involved both a narrator and a second person who transcribed the narrator's

6

story and then later prepared the account for publication. To authenticate the documents and then reach some judgment regarding their accuracy has required investigation into the career of each of these people. Further effort was necessary to place the texts of these documents securely within their proper historical context and to give them factual annotation. The process of research at times was a job of historical detective work, with results that may help to solve some minor mysteries in the history of the Northwest Coast during the early years of the nineteenth century.

The most intriguing of these mysteries involves the true historical identity of Timofei Tarakanov. His name appears at various places in the surviving records of the Russian American Company between 1803 and 1823. But, because of a repeated error, his first name and patronymic frequently have been confused. Often secondary accounts have called him Vasilii Petrovich Tarakanov. The false identity of this supposed Vasilii Tarakanov has been fixed so firmly in the historical literature that at first, when beginning to prepare these documents for publication, it seemed reasonable to suppose that two different Tarakanovs had worked for the Company in this era. But such a supposition led into a maze of contradictions when the attempt was made to distinguish the exploits of Timofei from those of the supposed Vasilii. The alternative conclusion, that the record referred only to one Tarakanov who somehow had been misidentified with two different names, also led to confusion on some crucial matters of detail.

These problems had their origin, it finally appeared, in a clear case of documentary fraud. The hoax was perpetrated about 1878 by Ivan Petrov, a Russian-born researcher and writer then in the employ of Hubert Howe Bancroft, the pioneer historian of California and the Pacific Coast. The appendix to this volume contains a detailed description of the fraud and discusses, point-by-point, the evidence dealing with Petrov's hoax.

To summarize the matter here, Petrov passed off on Bancroft a manuscript he claimed to have translated from a Russian original published at St. Petersburg in the *Morskoi Sbornik*, a naval journal. But the original cannot be found in that or any other source. The manuscript itself, now located in The Bancroft Library at the University of California, Berkeley, shows physical evidence of its fraudulent composition. In detail after detail, moreover, the account in the Petrov manuscript lacks verification or directly conflicts with the evidence of authentic contemporary documents.

The story in the manuscript demonstrates Petrov's gift for historical fantasy, a gift he exercised on other occasions as well. An account Tarakanov supposedly related to a Russian Orthodox missionary at Unalaska, the manuscript describes Vasilii's purported adventures in California and Hawaii. The main episode deals with his capture by the Spanish and his imprisonment by the Franciscans at some unnamed California mission, before he and a number of Aleut companions were liberated and returned to the Russian authorities.

Bancroft accepted this fiction as fact and incorporated it into both his *History of California* and *History of Alaska*. Other writers, relying on Bancroft's substantial authority, took the episode and the name of Vasilii Tarakanov from his publication. Still others made use of Petrov's original fraudulent document without pausing to give it their critical scrutiny. Finally, as an extension of the fraud, a number of writers have applied the name of the fictional Vasilii to the activities of the authentic, historical Timofei Tarakanov. Hence, in some secondary accounts it has been stated that Vasilii, not Timofei, sailed aboard the *Sv. Nikolai* in 1808. That mistake, traceable to Petrov's whimsy and Bancroft's gullibility, may now be set aside.

Once the confusion of identities is obviated, Timofei Osipovich Tarakanov emerges as an important figure among the employees of the Russian American Company during its early years. Born about 1780, he apparently received a rudimentary formal education. He was intelligent, more or less literate, and he could keep accounts, accomplishments that made him a valuable servant to the Company. In addition he gained a reputation for trustworthiness, sobriety, and resourcefulness that earned him the respect of Chief Manager Baranov and other Company officials. Probably he was one of those fur hunters enlisted by the Company in eastern Siberia and brought to America between 1799, when the Company was chartered, and 1803, when he unmistakably entered the historical record. Possibly he was one of the three Russians who survived an 1802 Tlingit attack on the Company's small outpost on Sitka Sound, St. Michael, shortly after Baranov had established that settlement.[3] The following year Tarakanov sailed to California for the first time, when Baranov ordered him aboard the Yankee ship *O'Cain* to hunt sea otters with a crew (*artel*) of Aleuts along the California coast. This voyage, governed by an agreement between Baranov and the ship's captain, Joseph O'Cain, is well known as the first Russian expedition to raid California's sea otter herds.[4]

After a brief hiatus in the record, Company correspondence plainly identifies Tarakanov in October of 1805 as a Karluk *baidarshchik* who was considered essential for further hunting expeditions.[5] This reference provides a further definition of his role. Karluk, on the northwest side of Kodiak Island, was a substantial native settlement that had been frequented by the Russians since the mid-1780s. The people of Karluk—properly classified as Kad'iaks or Koniagas—had come to depend heavily on the wages made by the men as sea otter hunters for the Russian American Company. Apparently Tarakanov was established well enough at Karluk to recruit these hunting parties and, we may infer, serve as the leader of their expeditions. Perhaps married to a Karluk woman, according to the custom of the country, he would be a translator, an intermediary, an expedition commander, and a sort of commercial patron for these men.

The following season, in 1806–07, Tarakanov led a crew of native sea otter hunters aboard the *Peacock*, another American ship that sailed to California under a partnership agreement between Baranov and its owners. The captain, Oliver Kimball, made Bodega Bay in northern California his base for a very successful hunt.[6]

Although we have no direct evidence, it is likely that early in 1808 Tarakanov joined the Company's hunting operations along the coast adjacent to New Arkhangel, the post that Baranov had built on Sitka Sound after recapturing the site of St. Michaels from the Tlingit. These 1808 operations were especially dangerous since the Russians and the Aleut hunters were challenging the men of the Tlingit nation in their own waters. Well-armed and not reconciled to the Russian and Aleut invaders who plundered their sea otter resources, the Tlingits were easily able to overpower and destroy any small groups of Russian and Aleut hunters caught in their skin baidarkas.

Tlingit opposition helped to convince Chief Manager Baranov that he should attempt to expand the Company's activities in the south. If he could establish Russian bases along the coasts of the Oregon Country and California, he would both bypass the Tlingit barrier and advance Russia's imperial frontier against the competition of the Spanish, British, and Yankees. Hence he outfitted the *Sv. Nikolai* in the fall of 1808 for a voyage down the coast, to trade and explore the region between Vancouver Island and the Columbia River.[7]

At Baranov's order, Tarakanov became the supercargo (*prikashchik*) on this voyage. In this position he was required to manage the Company's goods, conduct the trade with natives along the coast, direct the Russian and Aleut fur hunters aboard the ship, and safeguard in every way the Company's financial interests during the voyage. Only the ship's captain, Navigator Nikolai Isaakovich Bulygin, had a higher position. Tarakanov, when it was proper, carefully deferred to Bulygin's authority; but in the times of crisis after the expedition was cast ashore, as his own account shows, he did not hesitate to assume the responsibilities of leadership. His good sense, the force of his personality, and his strong will to survive, Tarakanov's narrative leads us to believe, made him a natural leader among his comrades.

Although surely he must have gained some local renown at New Arkhangel after his return from this ill-fated expedition, Tarakanov received from the Company scarcely any time to recuperate. In June 1810 he shipped aboard the *Isabella*, Captain Davis, to hunt sea otter once more in California, where he remained through the summer of 1811. After another hiatus in the record, we know that he returned to California still again in January of 1814 aboard the *Il'men*, and on this trip he apparently was assigned to remain at the newly founded Russian outpost, Ross Colony. He may have led a crew of sea otter hunters from Ross Colony traveling northward in baidarkas to Humboldt Bay during the summer of 1814. And, after rejecting the fraudulent account of his supposed capture by the Spanish in 1814 or 1815, we can establish his presence at Ross Colony through April of 1816. Then he again boarded the *Il'men*, expecting to return to New Arkhangel. Because of an accident to the ship when leaving the harbor at Bodega Bay, however, the captain instead made the safer voyage to the Hawaiian Islands.[8]

Tarakanov's adventures in Hawaii form a final chapter, so far as the available documents show, in his remarkable career. For nearly two years he had a leading part in the peculiar scheme of Dr. Georg Schaeffer, a German adventurer engaged by Chief Manager Baranov, to make the Hawaiian Islands a part of Russia's Pacific empire. A story told well by Richard Pierce in his book *Russia's Hawaiian Adventure*, this episode again brought forth Tarakanov's talent for leadership and his steadfast devotion to the interests of the Company. By February of 1818, according to the sources published by Pierce, Tarakanov had returned to New Arkhangel, only to have Baranov order him back to Hawaii on the Company's behalf.[9] Subsequently his name disappears from the historic record. Every student interested in the Pacific Coast and Russian America during these first two decades of the nineteenth century will welcome the appearance of additional evidence regarding this talented man and his extraordinary, nearly incredible career.

During the voyage of the *Sv. Nikolai*, Tarakanov kept a rough manuscript journal that he carried through the shipwreck, his flight, captivity, and return to New Arkhangel. The history of his narrative as a literary document only began really after his rescue in 1810. On his return he surrendered the journal to Chief Manager Baranov, who in turn brought it to the attention of Navy Captain (later Rear Admiral) Vasilii M. Golovnin, an outstanding figure in the Tsarist Navy of the nineteenth century.[10] Encouraged by Baranov, Golovnin became interested in the story of Tarakanov and his companions aboard the *Sv. Nikolai*. Since he had difficulty in understanding Tarakanov's rough journal, Golovnin explained later in his introduction to the narrative, he interviewed Tarakanov and a number of his shipmates in New Arkhangel. Then, from his journal and these interviews, Golovnin composed the narrative of Tarakanov's adventures in the Oregon Country.

In his introduction to the account, Golovnin demonstrated a sense of respect for historical detail. A person of critical ability, literary skill, and lively curiosity, he was concerned with accuracy and fidelity to the original. Because of Tarakanov's rough, unskilled style, he declared, it had been necessary to rewrite the journal completely. But, Golovnin claimed, "all the ideas and events I have retained exactly as they were described, without the slightest addition and without abridgment." The high quality of Golovnin's other works as author, translator, and editor lends credence to his claim. Substantiation by other sources, now including Ben Hobucket's Quileute tradition, makes it more certain that the narrative is accurate, not corrupted in any important way by Captain Golovnin.

If we consider that Tarakanov and Golovnin were jointly responsible for this project, they might be faulted only for a few errors of omission, easily explained by the circumstances in which the narrative was composed. As with many adventuring story tellers, Tarakanov and his comrades were inclined to magnify their accomplishments and play down their failures. Golovnin also was anxious to tell their story in part as a lesson for others, pointing out the hardihood and valor of these Russian seamen. Thus the account emphasizes the heroic quality of the Russians, with special attention to Tarakanov's special virtues. Plainly Tarakanov felt it necessary to justify his assumption of authority in the place of Navigator Bulygin. In addition, maybe due to Golovnin's influence, the published text makes a special plea for the justice of the Russians' behavior toward the native people. Tarakanov and Golovnin failed to explain, as the Hobucket narrative reveals, that during the winter after the shipwreck and before their surrender, the Russian party was continually beleaguered by the natives.

A single substantive mistake appears in the Golovnin publication, the result of geographical confusion by either Golovnin or (more likely) his literary executor. The title page, which the present volume produces in translation, states that the *Sv. Nikolai* wrecked "on the Island named Destruction by Vancouver." In fact, as stated earlier, the shipwreck site is just north of James Island and the mouth of the Quillayute River. Destruction Island, mentioned earlier in the account as the place where the ship first came close to disaster, lies some fourteen miles south of that point. Since Golovnin's narrative fixes the point exactly, the reference to Destruction Island was probably the addition of another, less careful hand than his.

As to style, Golovnin was disposed towards the dramatic. Tarakanov gave him a story replete with thrilling incidents and remarkable twists of fate. He did not ignore the literary opportunities in this material. The result was a work that well fits into the genre of nineteenth century frontier travel adventures, an international genre especially prominent in British and Anglo-American tales of personal experiences in the American West. This class of literature developed its own conventions and attitudes, many of which Golovnin adopted in a Russian form. To retain the style of this genre in translation, we have attempted to find appropriate English equivalents for the rather figurative, romantic language preferred by Golovnin.

With some critical heed to these matters of natural bias and literary style, Golovnin's version of the Tarakanov narrative may be regarded as an accurate historical and ethnographic source. As an editor, Golovnin did succeed in preserving the integrity of Taraknov's account in essential matters. Through his efforts we have available an honest, detailed, vivid description of the events that befell this Russian expedition on the isolated coast of the Oregon Country between November of 1808 and the spring of 1810.

The publication history of this work will interest some scholars. It appeared first in serial form with the title "Krushenie sudna Sv. Nikolaia, 1818 g." [The wreck of the St. Nicholas in 1818] in the *Severnyi Arkniv*, (vol. 4, Nos 21, 22), in 1822. After Golovnin's death his son published the narrative in a volume entitled *Opisanie primechatel'nykh korablekrushenii preterpennykh russkimi moreplavateliami cobrano i popolneno primechaniiami i poiasneniiami flota Kapitanom-Komandoram Golovninym* [*Description of remarkable shipwrecks suffered by Russian mariners, collected and amplified with notes and explanations by Navy Captain-Commander Golovnin*]. This volume appeared in St. Petersburg in 1853, with Tarakanov's narrative of the *Sv. Nikolai* shipwreck on pages 406–29. Twenty-one years later the entire volume appeared again as the fourth in a five-volume series entitled *Sochineniia i Perevody* [*Works and Translations*]. This last edition has been used as the source for the present translation. The modern Soviet edition of Golovnin's works, edited by I. P. Magidovich (Moscow and Leningrad, 1949), also included the Tarakanov narrative as it appeared in the 1874 edition.

One other Russian version of the narrative needs to be mentioned. In 1884, N. Bogomolov, a well-known writer, published in Moscow a thirty-page booklet with the title *V Plenu u Indeitsev. Instinnoe Proisshestvie (1808 g.). Iz Vospominanii Moriaka.* [*Held Captive by the Indians. A True Incident (1808). From the Reminiscences of a Seaman.*] The only known copy of the booklet is in the Lenin Library. Through the courtesy of that institution we obtained a microfilm copy. After making a careful translation, we must conclude that it certainly is not the original source the work purports to be. It is instead a piece of popular hackwork, baldly plagiarized from the earlier Golovnin edition. The author invented some small bits of dialogue, pretending to have interviewed Tarakanov at Sitka in the 1850s. But the text's structure, the information it contains, and even the smallest detail of incident make it quite evident that Bogomolov relied entirely upon the work of Golovnin as his direct source.

When the first Russian edition came out in serial form in 1822, the *St. Peterburgischer Zeitung* also printed a German translation (vol. 10, pp. 22–52). Four years later (1826) a first English translation appeared in the *Asiatic Journal* (vol. 18, pp. 245–53). A very loose translation, omitting much significant detail, this version fortunately gained no scholarly notice. Another English summary, based on Golovnin's 1853 edition, appeared in 1922. This publication, in effect a synopsis of the Tarakanov narrative, was the work of C. L. Andrews, who placed it in the *Washington Historical Quarterly*, (vol. 13, pp. 27–31). One more English version, possibly based on Andrews' work, formed part of Hector Chevigny's popular volume, *Russian*

America: The Great Alaskan Venture (New York, 1965; reprint ed., 1973).

In none of these editions, Russian, German, or English, has Tarakanov's narrative received a detailed scholarly examination. Captain Golovnin originally supplied the narrative with a series of annotations, explaining some terms that would be unfamiliar to readers in Russia and glossing certain of Tarakanov's remarks about Russian policy toward the native peoples. Most later editions simply copied these sketchy notes. The modern Soviet edition adds a few editorial comments that display no close knowledge of the geographical area or the historical circumstances in which the narrative is placed. The two modern English language versions, both incomplete translations, contain various inaccuracies. Moreover the Chevigny treatment, though longer and closer to Golovnin's text, is marred by the author's tendency to call on his imagination for details not found in the original or in any other documentary sources.

The history of the Quileute account of these events, conveyed from Ben Hobucket to Albert Reagan, has its own complications. Reagan served as a field officer for the U.S. Bureau of Indian Affairs at the Quileute Indian Reservation in Washington between 1905 and 1909. Born in Iowa in 1871, Reagan had been in the Indian Service since 1899, seeing duty first in New Mexico and South Dakota, meanwhile completing a master's degree at the University of Indiana. He was interested in American Indian ethnology, and so during his tenure among the Quileute he began a study of local mythology and legends. From native informants he collected a number of stories drawn from the oral literature of the Quileute and Hoh people.[11]

Among others, members of the Hobucket family at La Push assisted Reagan in his project. Then Ben Hobucket, an older man, specifically asked Reagan to record a tradition of the first coming of the white people to Quileute. Hobucket was ill with tuberculosis, Reagan later stated, and he was concerned that this particular story be recorded before his death. Hence, Reagan later wrote, "he asked that the account be put in print, with his

15

name, so that it would remain as part of the 'history' of his people."

The narrative that Hobucket gave to Reagan has the appearance of a tradition formed at least three generations prior to the time it was recorded. Hobucket knew about the captive woman who had lived with his family, though of course he had not known her personally. The account of her adventures he had received as a family tradition. The other events surrounding the shipwreck of the *Sv. Nikolai* he likewise had by tradition, at second or third hand.

Hobucket began his account with a conventional phrase, translated as "In the long, long ago. . . ," a phrase meant to indicate an indefinite point in the past. Such a convention is typical in the oral literature of the Quileute and many other peoples who did not maintain a calendric system of dating. It is not the same as the conventional "Once upon a time. . ." of the European fairytale. Instead, it indicates a real time that is earlier than the personal experience of the narrator, and earlier than any exact time reference that would be familiar to his audience.

Although the procedure of Reagan and Hobucket cannot be outlined with certainty, Hobucket no doubt told the narrative in the Quileute language. An original typescript of Reagan's article, deposited in the Washington State Library, Olympia, carries on its title page the notation that Gordon B. Hobucket, an assistant in the Indian school, served as interpreter for Reagan. Hence it is likely that as Ben Hobucket related his account, Reagan set down the translation given by Gordon Hobucket in a rough English version. Subsequently he must have reworked his rough copy and prepared a final draft, probably without returning to verify details of the translation either with Ben or Gordon Hobucket. It may be, indeed, that the work was not put into final form until many years later, long after Ben Hobucket's death. As with much of Reagan's work, his methods in this case were haphazard and his ideas about the topic not at all systematic. He did no background research at any time, only writing down what he thought Hobucket meant to say or should have said.

Reagan began publishing his Quileute and Hoh materials in early 1907, but the Hobucket account did not reach print until

1934, the year Reagan retired from the Indian Service. In the interim he had completed a Ph.D. degree at Stanford University (1925), and after his retirement he took an appointment as a special professor of anthropology at Brigham Young University. A prolific writer on many topics related to geology and natural history as well as Indian cultures, he was a fellow of the American Association for the Advancement of Science, and with his retirement he became active in the Utah Academy of Sciences.

To find subjects he might present to the semi-annual meetings of the Utah Academy, Reagan turned again to his work among the Quileute and Hoh a quarter century earlier. Ben Hobucket's story of the first white people among the Quileute he included in a collection of oral accounts that he entitled, with less than descriptive justice, "Some Traditions of the West Coast Indians." The account is republished here as it appeared in the 1934 *Proceedings of the Utah Academy of Sciences, Arts and Letters* (Provo, 1934), pages 86–89. Omitted here is Reagan's short introductory note, explaining the circumstances in which he was given the account, and also Reagan's few parenthetical additions to the text.

In comparison with Golovnin's treatment of the Tarakanov story, we must judge that Ben Hobucket found a less capable amanuensis in Albert Reagan. No doubt Hobucket's narrative tradition had suffered some loss of detail by the time he related the tradition to Reagan. There is no reason to believe, however, that the account had been corrupted. The narrative structure remained accurate; the description of events can now be verified at many points. Moreover the account retained passages of real descriptive power, indicating its origin in vivid experience. But plainly Reagan lacked some element of skill and understanding necessary for his task.

It was his intention, Reagan declared, to prepare a nearly literal translation of the native language, preserving the native idiom and viewpoint. Yet his published version is marred by an incongruity of language and an inconsistency of attitude, reflecting an editorial perception out of harmony with his sources. He calls the Hoh "savages," for example, and describes their actions as "frenzied." Apart from such a recurrence to the language of racism, there appears an intrusive invention of de-

17

tail, presumably for literary effect, that must have been the work of Reagan. It is impossible to believe, to cite one instance, that the narrative tradition contained such a sentence as this: "In an instant the ocean front was alive with savages." Surely Reagan is responsible for the addition of such language; and if so, we may believe that his natural genre was the melodrama of the dime novel.

At one critical point Reagan's editorial tinkering has a misleading effect. He makes the narrative say that the Hoh scalped a number of Russians at the time they tricked the Russian party into their boats in order to cross the Hoh River. The practice of scalping was altogether foreign to the Hoh and Quileute. Instead, as we learn from Tarakanov, these Russians, including Anna Petrovna Bulygin, were taken captive by the Hoh. Either Reagan misunderstood Hobucket on this matter, or he later misread his own notes; or perhaps he substituted a simpler, more stereotypical reading for the complications of the original account.

Aside from this one major error, the Hobucket narrative still survived rather well the perils of translation and Reagan's editorial treatment. So far as one may judge, it conveys the sense of the Quileute tradition regarding the wreck of the *Sv. Nikolai*. Then, without making an obvious transition, it proceeds to describe the experiences of the Russian and Aleut fugitives, based on the story told by the captured Aleut woman. This account covers those events from the point the Russian party first reached the Hoh village, through their winter spent upriver, until they returned downriver, made their escape attempt, and finally surrendered to the Quileutes. Missing from this version is the drama of Anna Petrovna Bulygin, Tarakanov's negotiations with the Makahs, and the surrender of Tarakanov, Bulygin, and a few others to the Makah people. But upon comparison, it is evident where these events should be fitted into the captive woman's narrative framework.

Together, the two accounts make it possible to deduce the identity of this woman. She was one of the two Aleut women aboard the *Sv. Nikolai* who, along with Tarakanov and the other Russian survivors, was later ransomed by Captain Brown and returned to New Arkhangel. This identification makes more

18

plausible the final sequence in Ben Hobucket's narrative tradition, which relates that a woman returned to their shores in another trading vessel and, in their own language, warned the Quileute to stay away from the ship. They would be carried off as slaves, this woman cried out, if they came aboard.[12] From this brief incident, otherwise unrecorded, we may guess that a cordial relationship grew up between this Aleut woman and the Quileute during the year or more she lived with Ben Hobucket's people.

When Albert Reagan took down this tradition, he could regard it as a curious item from the oral literature of the Quileute. A collector of the curious, he seems to have translated and edited the account in this spirit, making no effort towards historical verification of the episode. Once collated with the Tarakanov materials, this account assumes greater value as a historical source document. It is a record of unique origin, greatly enhancing our knowledge of the adventures that overtook the party shipwrecked from the *Sv. Nikolai*. The result is an intriguing double and even triple view of the same events, cutting across differences of language and culture. These sources, backed by other documentary evidence, make it possible to reconstruct a multi-dimensional history of this first Russian expedition to the Oregon Country.

When their ship was beached near the mouth of the Quillayute River, the Russian party landed in a region in which they found survival difficult. This isolated country, the western, seaward side of the Olympic Peninsula, is a land of dense hemlock forest, interspersed with spruce and cedar inland from the coast. Thick tangles of vines and brush overgrow the forest floor, and immense stands of ferns fill the forest openings. Weather fronts move into this area from the North Pacific, bringing frequent storms and super-abundant rainfall during most of the year. To the interior the Olympic Mountains rise nearly 8,000 feet, forming a weather barrier that makes this country a classic rainforest environment. Annual rainfall averages between 110 and 120 inches, making it one of the wettest locations in North America. Some snow usually falls during the winter, but only rarely does it become deep at the lower elevations.

A number of good-sized rivers drain the area, originating on the slopes of Mt. Olympus and flowing westward into the Pacific. Two of these, the Soleduck and Bogachiel, combine to form the Quillayute River, which enters the ocean about thirty miles south of Cape Flattery. Another major stream, the Hoh River, enters the Pacific fifteen miles farther to the south. Still farther down the coast, the Queets River and the Quinault River trace parallel courses from Mt. Olympus southwest to the ocean. These rivers and the sea formed the main lines of communication through a country difficult to traverse even for those familiar with its terrain.

The forbidding aspect of this country when viewed from the sea was enough to cause trepidation in honest sailors. John Meares, a British seaman, penned a striking description when he coasted southward from Tatoosh Island on a trading voyage in the summer of 1788. "The appearance of the land," Meares wrote, "was wild in the extreme—immense forest covered the whole of it within our sight, down to the very beach, which was lofty and cragged, and against which the sea dashed with fearful rage. The shore was lined with rocks and rocky inlets, nor could we perceive any bay or inlet that seemed to promise the least security to the smallest vessel." [13]

By the time of the *Sv. Nikolai*'s expedition, the native people of this country had already gained among Europeans a reputation for their bellicosity and fierce courage. The Quileute and Hoh, native to the territory drained by the Quillayute and Hoh rivers, were closely related; members of the Chimakum linguistic family, they had once formed a single ethnographic community, and their social ties remained close. These people lived in small settlements along the rivers and larger creeks, with their largest communities located on the coast at the mouths of the rivers. Their most abundant food was salmon, but they also ate quantities of smelt, cod, halibut, steelhead, and many varieties of shellfish. Their plant foods included fern roots, camas, and at least a dozen different kinds of berries that grew along the streams. They were notable hunters, taking seals, sea lions, and sea otters on the ocean, and on land such animals as elk, black bear, deer, bighorn sheep, and mountain goats from the forest and interior mountain areas. [14]

Skilled in the use of weapons, these people did not lightly tolerate intruders in their homelands, and they were accustomed to fighting. Frequently they battled with the Makah, who lived to the north, and less frequently with the Nootka, whose home country was farther northward, along the west coast of Vancouver Island. These northern nations raided the Quileute and Hoh, coming by sea in their great war canoes; and the Quileute and Hoh warriors launched their own counter-raids. In these battles the victors could gain prestige and enhance their wealth by taking captives who would be kept as family servants or slaves, or who might either be given away or sold. Captives were regarded as a type of property in a society whose members had great respect for propertied wealth. Ownership of such captives, whether men, women, or children, brought honor to the owner and his family. The life of the captive might be more or less difficult, the captive's treatment more or less harsh, according to the character and the whim of a master.

Since their enemies made raids for captives just as they did, the Quileute and Hoh were vigilant to defend their shores against all strangers. The first Europeans to visit this coast had learned the peril. In 1775 a Spanish party from the schooner *Sonora* was ambushed and destroyed when they put ashore to get water. In all likelihood this episode occurred in the lee of Cape Elizabeth, just below the mouth of the Quinault River, some twenty-two miles south of Destruction Island and the Hoh River. Twelve years later a British ship sailing under Austrian colors, the *Imperial Eagle*, lost a boat crew at the mouth of the Hoh River, where the mate, the purser, and four seamen were slain by native people. After these incidents the British and American traders came to regard the inhabitants of the coast south of Cape Flattery as a particularly treacherous race, although the deceit and violence increasingly practiced by these profit-hungry traders made them poor models of honorable conduct for their native clients.[15]

North of the Quileute and Hoh lived the Makah, people of a separate cultural community who made their homes in the Cape Flattery and Neah Bay region, along the Straits of Juan de Fuca. They were members of the Wakashan linguistic family, closely related to the Nootka on southern Vancouver Island.

Their way of life resembled in many particulars the Quileute and Hoh; but their more elaborate ceremonies, their highly developed sense of social hierarchy, and their claims to aristocratic distinctions marked the Makah as a people even more concerned with wealth, status, and high prestige than their neighbors to the south. The Makah and Nootka enjoyed a particular fame as whale hunters, demonstrating in this dangerous enterprise a skill and daring unmatched on the Northwest Coast. In addition, as Tarakanov and his shipmates discovered, these people took a large role in the trade for captives and slaves that prevailed along the entire Northwest Coast.[16]

One Makah individual has a special place in Timofei Tarakanov's narrative: the man who became Tarakanov's master and later arranged the rescue of the Russian captives. He is called Yutramaki by Tarakanov. Beyond doubt this man is the same person whose name appears elsewhere among contemporary sources as Machee Ulatilla or Utillah. Fortunately for editorial purposes, we have a rather detailed description of this man in the published narrative of John Jewett, the survivor of a Nootka attack on the ship *Boston* in 1804, who was held captive by the Nootka *tyee* (or chief) Maquinna. Jewett calls this man Machee Ulatilla, speaks of him as chief of the "Klaizzarts," a contemporary name for the Makah, and describes him in these words:

> This chief, who could speak tolerable English, had much more the appearance of a civilized man than any of the savages that I saw. He appeared to be about thirty, was rather small in person, but extremely well formed, with a skin almost as fair as that of an European, good features, and a countenance expressive of candor and amiableness, and which was almost always brightened with a smile. He was much neater both in dress and person than any of the other chiefs, seldom wearing paint, except upon his eye-brows, which, after the custom of his country, were plucked out, and [he had] a few strips of the *pelpelth* [tattoo] on the lower part of his face. He always treated me

22

with much kindness, was fond of conversing with me in English and in his own language, asking me many questions relative to my country, its manners, customs &c, and appeared to take a strong interest in my fate, telling me, that if he could persuade Macquinna to part with me, he would put me on board the first ship that came to his country; a promise, which, from his subsequent conduct, I have good reason to think he would have performed.[17]

Although Machee Ulatilla failed in his efforts to purchase Jewett from Macquinna, in July of 1805 he did carry a letter from Jewett to a Yankee trading ship off Cape Flattery, the brig *Lydia* under Captain Samuel Hill, and Captain Hill then rescued Jewett by a combination of persuasion, guile, and force. The manuscript diary of Captain Hill, found in the Manuscripts Division of the New York Public Library, coincides with Jewett's account and helps to corroborate the identification of this man as the same *tyee* who became Timofei Tarakanov's master four years later.[18]

John Jewett's description of this man, supported by the evidence of Tarakanov's narrative, gives rise to an additional suggestion. It is possible, even likely, that Yutramaki or Machee Ulatillah was the son of an earlier European visitor to this coast. His light skin color, his great curiosity about the Europeans and their ways, his interest in their languages and customs, the European manner of dress that he affected, and his eagerness to help the stranded or captured Europeans return to their homeland; all these characteristics suggest strongly that Yutramaki, like no other Makah or Nootka person of the era, felt a deep and genuine concern for these foreigners. It was a concern that might well have been motivated by a consciousness of his own European paternity. His approximate age, if Jewett was a good judge, dates his birth to the period of earliest European exploration along these shores.

To follow the suggestion a step further, the documents prove it unlikely that the first Spanish explorers made any sexual alliances with native women in the Oregon Country. Opportunity seems to have been lacking during the 1774 visit of

Pérez aboard the *Santiago*, while Bodega's expedition the following year aboard the *Sonora* did not put ashore in this area.[19]

When Captain James Cook anchored in Nootka Sound in March and April of 1778, his "young gentlemen," the midshipmen aboard the *Discovery* and *Resolution*, did purchase from some native fathers the sexual favors of their daughters. Most likely it was the Haida people, visitors to Cook's ships from farther north, and not the Nootka or the Makah, who entered this trade to earn the shiny pewter plates that Cook's midshipmen bartered away. No record exists of any consequences from these relations.[20]

After Cook's voyage, English trading ships began to arrive on the Northwest Coast in 1785 and 1786, coming from Canton to enter the sea otter trade. One of the first ships to reach Nootka Sound was the *Captain Cook*, Henry Laurie master, a voyage of interest because Laurie left on shore his ship's surgeon. This person, an Irishman, was quite ill when the ship came to Nootka in June of 1786. He begged permission to remain behind, either to die or recuperate. Captain Laurie permitted him to stay, making him the first European sojourner at Nootka Sound. The name of this man was John McKay or MacCay or McKey.[21]

Not only did McKay recover, we know from various accounts that he went thoroughly native, took a wife, and became for one season a respected guest among the Nootka people. In August 1787, when opportunity allowed, he decided to leave aboard the *Imperial Eagle*. Although John Meares claimed to have seen the journal McKay kept during his stay at Nootka, that valuable document and McKay himself disappeared from view when the *Imperial Eagle* returned to Canton in November.

Although skeptics will not find the case established beyond all reasonable doubt, it is certainly possible that Yutramaki or Machee Ulatillah was the son of John McKay and his native wife. In Cook's time the Nootka had proved themselves little inclined to promote the union of their women with strangers. McKay's wife may well have been a captive living among the Nootka, either a Makah or from some other people. If a Makah, we might suppose she then returned home to raise the child left her by McKay. An alien paternity would have been no bar-

24

rier to this son's attainment of high status among the Makah, since these people recognized the inheritance of rank through the maternal line. The similarity in names, the personal details, and many of the circumstances urge such a conclusion. If so, Jewett estimated his age wrong by some ten or twelve years— the strongest evidence against this conclusion. But Jewett was young and inexperienced himself. He could have been wrong about the man's age.

Setting aside this possibility, it remains certain that Yutramaki was an unusual person among the Makah in the time of Jewett and Tarakanov. With his imitation of European ways and his eagerness to aid those Europeans who came into native hands, he must have seemed to all who met him a distinctive, extraordinary figure. When Anna Petrovna Bulygin told her husband, along with Tarakanov and the others, to surrender and accept the protection of Yutramaki, she had good reason for her proposal. As with John Jewett before them, Tarakanov and his companions would finally have this man to thank for their rescue.

The Tarakanov and Hobucket narratives offer more than a tale of frontier adventure. They are significant in the wider history of international rivalry over the Oregon County during the era between the American Revolution and the end of the Napoleonic Wars. After the Pérez voyage of 1774 and the Hezeta and Bodega expedition of 1775, Spain asserted an exclusive claim to the Northwest Coast as far north as Bucareli Sound, on the west coast of Prince of Wales Island. Great Britain entered the area as a serious rival with the third voyage of Captain James Cook, who proceeded from Nootka northward to Prince William Sound and Cook Inlet on the Alaskan coast, thence to Unalaska and the Bering Sea during the summer and early fall of 1778. When Cook's ships returned to England in 1780, after Cook's death in Hawaii, they brought news of an abundant trade for sea otters on the Northwest Coast and a rich market for these pelts at Canton. With this information, British and Yankee merchants began an era of sharp competition for the sea otter trade with the peoples of the Northwest Coast. The Spanish briefly attempted to repulse this challenge; but in 1790 the Spanish government signed the Nootka Convention, in effect opening up the coastal waters north of California to the commerce of all nations.[22]

The United States and Great Britain established formal claims to the Oregon Country soon after the Nootka Convention. On 16 May 1792 Captain Robert Gray, a Yankee shipmaster in the sea otter trade, brought his ship the *Columbia Rediviva* across the bar of the great river which he named the Columbia in honor of his vessel, thus laying the basis for an American claim by virtue of discovery. A few weeks later Captain George Vancouver, a commissioned officer in the British navy, sent Lieutenant William Broughton and his ship the *Chatham* across the bar of the Columbia, and Lieutenant Broughton took a ship's boat more than ninety miles upriver. This accomplishment, along with Vancouver's detailed survey of Puget Sound waters, gave Britain a case for title to the Oregon Country by reason of exploration.

Overland expeditions bolstered these claims for both nations. On behalf of Great Britain, Alexander Mackenzie, a trader for the North West Company, led a party to the Pacific in July 1793, coming overland from Lake Athabaska by way of the Peace River and the Bella Coola River. The British were slow to follow up Mackenzie's exploit, allowing the United States to take the initiative in 1803 with the purchase of the Louisiana Territory and, beginning the same year, the overland expedition of Captains Meriwether Lewis and William Clark. This expedition, perhaps the most celebrated exploration since the voyages of James Cook, reached the mouth of the Columbia River in November 1805, nearly eighteen months after the two captains and their men had started up the Missouri River from St. Louis. They spent the winter at Fort Clatsop on the Columbia, then left for the return trip in March of 1806. When they returned safely to St. Louis late that same year, Lewis and Clark had given the United States a vastly improved position in later negotiations over the Oregon Country.

Russian interest in this area developed some time after the British and the Americans had fixed their initial claims. For more than half a century, since the 1741 second expedition of Vitus Bering and Aleksei Chirikov, Russian merchants and their crews of fur hunters had been raiding the vast sea otter and fur seal populations of the Aleutian Islands, Unalaska, and the Kodiak region. To bring this commerce under a systematic, centralized management, the Russian imperial government chartered the Russian American Company in 1799, granting the Company a monopoly right to trade, hunt, explore, and settle all the territory from the Bering Straits along the Alaskan coast and southward toward the "South Sea." Under this authority Aleksandr Baranov, the untutored commercial genius who directed all Company affairs in North America, first consolidated the Company's business at Kodiak, then established a new post on Sitka Island to extend hunting activities and give the Company better harbor facilities.[23]

An opportunist, Baranov seized his first chance to send Company sea otter hunters southward to California in 1803. Two years later, the same year that Lewis and Clark reached the Pacific, Baranov's expansive ambitions were stimulated by the American tour of Chamberlain Nikolai Rezanov, a high-ranking official in the government of Tsar Aleksandr and a member of the board of directors of the Russian American Company. Chamberlain Rezanov was an aggressive proponent of Russian imperialism. He encouraged the chief manager to challenge the claims of Spain, Great Britain, and the United States in the Oregon Country, for he saw profitable commercial prospects in that direction. Rezanov's vision, indeed, was even grander. By extending a series of posts from the Kurile Islands and Kamchatka to Sitka, Nootka, and southward to San Francisco Bay— including possibly a depot in the Hawaiian Islands—the Tsar's government could become a dominant power on the Pacific.

Rezanov's promotion of an expansionist strategy was cut short by his accidental death in 1806, when he was returning from America to St. Petersburg. But the encouragement he had given to Baranov prompted the chief manager to make plans for advancing Russian enterprise in California and the Oregon Country.

By 1808 the international situation encouraged Baranov's belief that the Russian American Company might preempt the commerce of the Pacific, gaining for the Tsar a strong position in the diplomatic struggle over the Northwest Coast. The British, allied with Russia, were locked in a desperate war against the France of Napoleon Bonaparte. Britain's maritime trade on the Northwest Coast had become a casualty of war. The Spanish government, its hold already slipping on an empire too immense for its enfeebled bureaucracy to rule, was made a captive of the Bonaparte regime, with Napoleon's brother Joseph seated on the Spanish throne. The United States meanwhile found its maritime trade a victim of British blockades and French confiscations. In an attempt to compel the warring powers to respect American trading rights, President Jefferson pushed through Congress the Embargo Act late in 1807. This measure, which forbade American ships to sail for foreign ports, soon proved an unmitigated disaster for America's mercantile economy.

As a result of these wartime circumstances, British and American traders nearly disappeared from the Northwest Coast. Only three American ships and one British ship were carrying on this trade in 1808, compared with a total of twenty-three ships under British and American colors in 1801 and seventeen in 1802. Rich cargos could still be taken; one ship, the *Pearl* of Boston, reportedly obtained 6,000 skins in a voyage of 1808–09. And though such slaughter was rapidly decimating the sea otter herds, there was a growing interest in beaver pelts, elk skins, and the furs of other land mammals that also found markets in China and Europe.[24]

Baranov's expansionist plans were always hampered by a lack of resources, and especially a shortage of suitable ships in Russian America. The *Sv. Nikolai* was a small schooner that he had acquired in a roundabout manner. In 1806, when Timofei Tarakanov was sailing to California with a group of Aleut sea otter hunters aboard the *Peacock*, Baranov again put a similar group aboard the *O'Cain* under the command of Pavl Slobodchikov. The *O'Cain* sailed south to the island of Cedros, off Baja California, for its hunt. There Slobodchikov quarreled violently with the shipmaster and part owner, Jonathan Winship, Jr., and left the ship. For 150 sea otter skins, his crew's share of the *O'Cain's* hunt, he purchased there a small ship that he named the *Sv. Nikolai*. Very likely this was a ship built in Hawaii for King Kamehameha I and christened the *Tamana* that had been purchased later by two Americans and sailed to Baja California.

28

With a makeshift crew of three Hawaiians and three Americans, Slobodchikov sailed the *Sv. Nikolai* back to Hawaii, then returned to New Arkhangel in August 1807, three months ahead of Captain Winship.[25]

That same year Baranov purchased another ship, the British brig *Myrtle*, which he renamed the *Kad'iak* and put into service with the *Sv. Nikolai* along the Northwest Coast. These two ships helped protect the expeditions of baidarka hunters in Tlingit territory during the first part of 1808. The force returned in July with a cargo of 1,700 sea otter skins; but the leaders had not been able to make a trade agreement with the Tlingit.

It was then Baranov determined to bypass the Tlingit and direct his energies toward the Oregon Country and California. He outfitted the *Sv. Nikolai* for a voyage that would chart the coastline, since the Russians lacked good maps of the shore south of Nootka Sound. As Chamberlain Rezanov had earlier planned, Baranov hoped the expedition would find a good site for a Russian fort and trading establishment somewhere near the mouth of the Columbia River. To help meet the expenses of the expedition, Baranov expected the ship to trade with the natives for sea otter and other peltry. Accordingly, he put aboard a supply of trade beads, imitation pearls, and similar goods, consigned to the care of Timofei Tarakanov. Finally Baranov directed the commander, Navigator Bulygin, to rendezvous with the *Kad'iak* at Gray's Harbor, where Bulygin would report the result of his reconnaissance to Baranov's most trusted assistant, Ivan Kuskov. The *Sv. Nikolai* might then join the *Kad'iak* on a voyage to California under Kuskov's supervision.[26]

The wreck of the *Sv. Nikolai* and the failure of the expedition came, of course, as a sharp setback to Baranov's plans. Not only did he lose valuable men and a full cargo on this voyage, he lost one of the few ships that could carry out the expeditions necessary for his long-range strategy. Still more important, he lost a crucial time advantage. By 1810, when Tarakanov and his surviving shipmates returned to New Arkhangel, both the British and the American fur traders had advanced their own plans for occupation of the Oregon Country. For the British North West Company, David Thompson was establishing a series of posts on the headwaters of the Columbia, on the Kootenay River, and on Lake Pend d'Oreille, and in 1811 he pushed his explorations down the Columbia to its mouth. Before Thompson's arrival, the advance force of John Jacob Astor's Pacific Fur Company had already arrived on the lower Columbia and begun the construction of the Astoria post. Astor, long interested in the maritime trade along the Northwest Coast, now meant to engross the fur business of the Oregon Country, excluding the British and carrying goods under contract to the Russian American Company.

With these movements by the British and the Americans, Russia's strategic moment passed and the struggle for the Oregon Country became an issue between the subjects of Great Britain and the citizens of the United States. Baranov apparently did not regret the missed opportunity. The Oregon Country, so far as he might judge, could supply little that the Russians needed for their Alaskan colony. Tarakanov and his shipmates had not found a good harbor. They did not discover rich, untapped fur resources. Nor did they meet any Indian nations eager to do the Russians' bidding as clients of the Company. Above all, Oregon gave to these Russians no hint of its promise as a source of agricultural foodstuffs. Although the Russian American colony was rich in sea otter and other valuable peltry, as well as fish and seals, the colonists were desperately short of flour and farm produce. The voyage of the *Sv. Nikolai* and Russia's other coastal expeditions could not reveal the fertile, open farmlands of the interior country to the managers of the Russian American enterprise. Neither Baranov nor his successors took any further real interest in the Oregon Country after 1810.

The Company's expansionist energies instead turned mainly toward California, where Ivan Kuskov founded Ross Colony in 1812. The Russians laid claim to a serviceable harbor at Bodega Bay and built Ross Fort a few miles to the north, making it the base for their operations on the farther frontier of Spain's American empire. Although never a truly profitable operation, Ross Colony was maintained by the company until 1841, mainly because of its importance as the staging point for a large trade with the Spanish missionaries and colonists in California. This trade, often clandestine, supplied the Russians in Alaska with fresh breadstuffs, wheat, wine, beef, and other food they lacked. For a generation, Ross Colony became an important outpost of Russian influence in America.[27]

In this historical context, the disastrous voyage of Timofei Tarakanov and his companions aboard the *Sv. Nikolai* may be thought less a total failure than it seems at first appraisal. The survivors were able to give Chief Manager Baranov a detailed description of the country they had seen and the native peoples among whom they had lived. This information, negative in character, pointed the Russian enterprise toward California, where the Company's agents were able to gain advantages they could not have realized in the Oregon Country. And, for another long period, the native peoples of the region visited by the shipwrecked expedition, the Quileute, the Hoh, and the Makah, were able to enjoy their isolation and relative immunity from the direct onslaught of Euro-American commercial civilization.

One last matter remains for assessment. What effects, we should ask, did the experiences of 1808−10 have on the lives of those individuals who were directly involved? Here is an episode virtually unique in the annals of the Russian American Company and in the record of native relations with the Russians and their Aleut work force, unique because it affords us a direct, close view of the lives of ordinary people on this remote frontier. What insights then can we gain regarding these folk, Northwest Coast natives, Aleuts, and Russians—humble souls by history's magisterial standards—through the events at that time and place?

While a great part of the answer must remain conjecture, a few points stand out clearly. For the Hoh and the Makah, the wreck of the *Sv. Nikolai* and the ensuing episodes were exceptional, yet they tried to fit them all smoothly into the patterns of their traditional ways. They treated the Russians and the Aleuts first as an invading force, then as a group to be duped, caught at disadvantage, captured or destroyed. But finally, after the marooned fur hunters ceased to be a threat, they treated these outlanders as individuals. They saw them as men and women with different personalities and different talents. Some, like Navi-

31

gator Bulygin, they could view as pitifully inept. Others, like Timofei Tarakanov in particular, they came to respect and honor for their skills and their ideas—for their alien but admirable genius. There could be left in Russia, they said to Tarakanov, few such geniuses. And there were others, like the Aleut woman who came to live with the Hobucket family, whom the native people simply accepted, for a time merging these strangers completely into their own society. The documents speak clearly of close, warm friendships formed—between Yutramaki and Tarakanov, and between the Aleut woman and the Hobucket family. Anna Petrovna Bulygin, to her husband's astonishment, commended in admiring terms the Makah man who had become her master, who had fed her, protected her and cared well for her after her capture. As for Yutramaki, she insisted, he was a good man and would keep his word to help the Russians, as indeed he did.

Personal accounts, the Tarakanov and Hobucket narratives give us statements of honest responses and uncloyed sentiments. They are testimony to humane qualities that reach across the barriers of language, culture, race, and time. We see these qualities fully developed in the closing episodes. Consider, for example, the care taken by Yutramaki to bring Tarakanov and all his surviving companions safely aboard *Lydia*. Consider as well the stubborn efforts of Captain Brown to manage the return of all the Russian and Aleut captives, but to do so without force and violence, and without making threats against those particular natives who had best looked after Tarakanov and his compatriots. These humane qualities certainly echo loudly at the end of the Hobucket narrative, in the story of the Aleut woman who warned the Quileute against coming aboard the slave ship, in the name of the god of the white man and of their own gods, Kwattee and Sekahtil.

Attention may be directed to the reluctance of some of the Makah and Quileute people to part with their Russian and Aleut captives. Was it a matter of commercial policy, or may it have been instead another indication of an emotional tie reluctantly broken? In this same vein, we might speculate upon the fate of apprentice Filip Kotel'nikov. Why did he never return? Was he perhaps the first young man of Russian origin to adopt thoroughly and permanently the native way of life in this frontier region? It often happened elsewhere.[28] Did he and his descendants perhaps live thenceforth among the Chinook or other Columbia River peoples? It would be satisfying to know.

More than the rest, what about our central figure, Tarakanov himself? What did his experience in the Oregon Country mean to this low-born company man? About this question we can reach a few definite conclusions. At the outset of the voyage Tarakanov was already a person who had gained stature among his peers by virtue of his personal accomplishments. The career that we can reconstruct prior to 1808 shows a pattern of upward achievement, capped by his designation as the Company's *prikashchik* or supercargo aboard the *Sv. Nikolai*. Other men would follow him, and the company could trust him.

Something more happened, the documents clearly argue, after the *Sv. Nikolai* went aground. Timofei Tarakanov rose in stature as his superior, Navigator Bulygin, lost his will to lead and surrendered control of the situation. When Bulygin declared that he could no longer carry on his appointed role, all agreed that Tarakanov must take command. Everyone expressed themselves out loud; then Bulygin wrote up a statement in pencil on some scrap of paper that he signed, and after him so did all the others who knew how to write. (What a prize it would be to find that scrap among the documents in some overlooked archives file.) The importance of the moment to Tarakanov, this humble soul, seems to shine forth across the intervening years. Made in an hour of misfortune, as the account says, that choice appears wise in retrospect. It must have seemed especially so a few days later when Tarakanov refused Bulygin's attempt to reassert his authority as commander, just so he could trade the group's few remaining guns to the natives in exchange for his wife.

And what kind of commander did Tarakanov become? Certainly he was no little tsar in the authoritarian model of Russia's aristocratic elite. Nor did he emulate the rages and emotional outbursts that Chief Manager Baranov often mixed into his leadership techniques. Nor did he follow the rash methods of

33

Navigator Bulygin, whose lack of foresight and snap decisions seem often to have made worse the calamities that beset his small ship and its people.

Tarakanov's command style was one of discussion and informed assent, a style that hoped to achieve among the party a consensus on all critical issues. He sought no democracy, in which the majority might claim its right to compel a dissenting minority to follow their single course of action. When the party at last divided, split by a difference of opinion on a life or death decision, Tarakanov and all the rest hugged and wept and parted like brothers, saying farewell.

This man's style of leadership suggests the methods of the Aleut native *toyon*, a leadership based upon full community participation, confidence, and support. It was leadership by proved ability and tested judgment, revocable instantly at the moment that either ability or judgment failed to command the community's approval. The style that worked for a Northwest Coast *toyon*, let it be added, seems remarkably like that of the Russian peasant commune. It was the style by which both these associations among humble people had managed their affairs presumably for centuries. It was the style of the free folk community in two parallel cultural traditions.

Tarakanov gained added stature the first weeks following the wreck of the *Sv. Nikolai*, and he did not let it slip away. After his capture the Makah soon recognized his abilities, making him a *starshina* in effect, giving him appropriate recognition and status in terms of their own culture. Later, as we know from other documents, Tarakanov became without question the leader of the Russian force in Hawaii, where popular consent gave him command on behalf of all his companions. Subsequently he either ordered away the discredited Dr. Schaeffer or suggested most persuasively that the ambitious physician, intent upon a grandiose chimera, resign his post and leave the islands. Whatever the case, Tarakanov demonstrated superb tact and diplomatic expertise in this instance, succeeding in his relations with the Hawaiian royalty where men of higher rank had failed. In our final documentary glimpse of Tarakanov, Chief Manager Baranov affirmed his leadership role, designating him as the Company's expert agent to clear up the Hawaiian mess that Dr. Schaeffer had left behind.

From these documents we may trace the account of an ordinary man's advance. Timofei Tarakanov, during the events chronicled in his narrative, seems to have moved through a decisive time in his own history. Legally a *promyshlennik* and in fact scarcely more than an indentured employee when history meets him, he rose to become a free man of independent opinions and confident action. He remained a servant of the Russian American Company; but, so far as a person of his origins could achieve it, he became an individual of recognized stature, a leader, a success in that most difficult, dangerous, and demanding of trades, the profession of a Russian fur hunter in frontier America. Supported then by his peers, Russian and Aleut, and rewarded by Aleksandr Baranov, he must have felt it an honor indeed to be recognized as the Company's agent and spokesman, a person of great value to the organization that represented all Russia in North America. It was a substantial heritage that Timofei Tarakanov could pass on to the infant son whose birth we find recorded at New Arkhangel in 1819, written in the register of the Russian Orthodox Church. Did that son, we would ultimately like to know, grow to appreciate his father's accomplishments; did he build upon them during his own life?

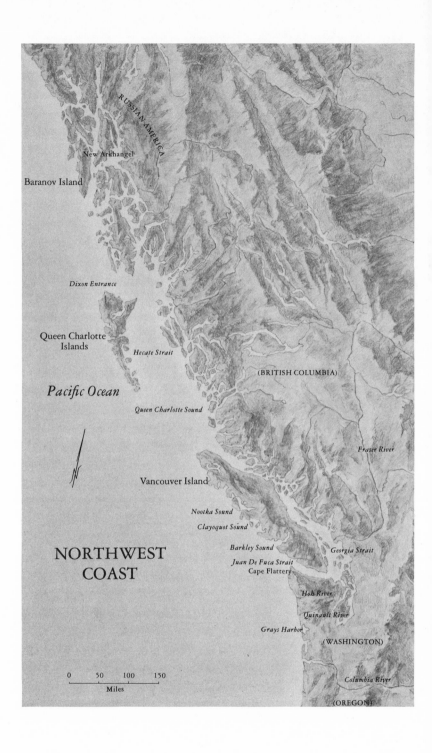

RUSSIAN AMERICA

New Arkhangel

Baranov Island

Dixon Entrance

Queen Charlotte
Islands

Hecate Strait

(BRITISH COLUMBIA)

Pacific Ocean

Queen Charlotte Sound

Fraser River

N

Vancouver Island

Nootka Sound

Clayoquot Sound

**NORTHWEST
COAST**

Barkley Sound

Georgia Strait

Juan De Fuca Strait
Cape Flattery

Hoh River

Quinault River

Grays Harbor

(WASHINGTON)

| 0 | 50 | 100 | 150 |

Miles

Columbia River

(OREGON)

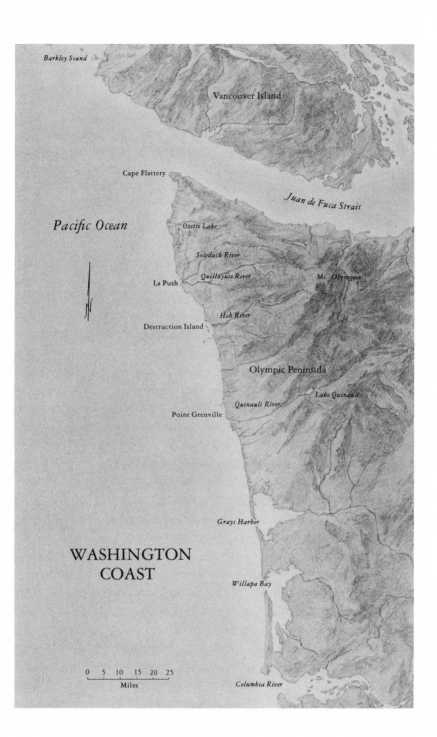

Barkley Sound

Vancouver Island

Cape Flattery

Juan de Fuca Strait

Pacific Ocean

Ozette Lake

Soleduck River

Quillayute River

Mt. Olympus

La Push

Hob River

Destruction Island

Olympic Peninsula

Lake Quinault

Quinault River

Point Grenville

Grays Harbor

WASHINGTON
COAST

Willapa Bay

0   5   10   15   20   25
Miles

Columbia River

37

The "interview" with Anna Bulygin

THE WRECK OF THE *Sv. NIKOLAI*

The Narrative of
Timofei Tarakanov

*The Wreck of the Russian-American Company Ship
Sv. Nikolai, under the command of Navigator Bulygin,
on November 1, 1808 on the Northwest Coast of America
at Approximately 47-1/2 N. Latitude on the Island
named Destruction Island by Vancouver*

English Translation by Alton S. Donnelly
from the Russian Edition by
Navy Captain-Commander Vasilii Mikhailovich Golovnin,
in *Words and Translation*
Volume 4 (St. Petersburg, 1874) pp. 406-28

Russian
Editor's Preface

I n 1810 while I was in America, I received from the Directory of the [Russian American] Company, College Councillor Baranov, a journal in which this shipwreck was described by one of the officers who sailed on the lost ship.[1] This officer, Timofei Tarakanov, was a capable seaman, well acquainted with navigation. He was, as they say, a skilled and upright man, although with little education. In order to understand his journal, therefore, on several occasions I found it necessary to call on him and the other *promyshlenniks* who were with him, to clarify the obscure and incomprehensible passages. Their account is extremely interesting; and though, with respect to the shipwreck itself, their actions failed to demonstrate the skill and steadfastness that might serve as a model worthy of imitation, subsequently these Russians showed their spirit and strong character in the most favorable light. Their remarks on the savages [*dikari*] of the Northwest Coast of America are also most interesting, particularly since these people are still little known to geographers.

For these reasons, with an intent to instruct and enlighten the reader, I have decided to provide, one might say, a translation of the whole of Tarakanov's journal. His style I have changed completely, but all the ideas and events I have retained exactly as they were described, without the slightest addition and without abridgment. Tarakanov always speaks of himself in the first person, and in this version of the narrative I have followed the same practice.

The Narrative of
Timofei Tarakanov

The Company brig *Sv. Nikolai*, on which I sailed in the position of supercargo, was under the command of Navy Navigator Bulygin, dispatched to the coast of New Albion [Oregon] under a special commission from the chief manager of the colonies. We departed [from New Arkhangel] on September 29, 1808, and about the 10th of October approached the Cape of Juan de Fuca, which lies at 48° 22' N. Latitude.[2] Here a calm held us up four days. Then a light westerly breeze began to blow, bringing us near the shore to the south, which we charted on the maps and added to our notes. During the night we usually moved out from the shore somewhat, then during the day moved in very close.

At this time many of the natives came out to us in their canoes. Sometimes the number of boats at the ship's side reached several dozen and even up to a hundred. The canoes were not very large. A few might seat approximately ten, but most held only three or four persons.[3] Nevertheless we were cautious, and never allowed more than three of the natives aboard our ship at any one time. This precaution seemed all the more essential to us because they were armed. Many even had firearms, while the others carried arrows made of deer horn, iron spears without shafts, and bone spikes fitted on long shafts. The latter were similar to our two-pronged pitchforks. In addition they had a particular kind of weapon made of whalebone, shaped like a chopping knife or a Turkish saber about a half *arshin* [14 inches] in length, two and a half *diums* [2 1/2 inches] in breadth, a quarter *dium* thick and with both edges blunt. At

41

first we could not imagine the purpose such a weapon might serve, but afterwards we learned that they were used on the night attacks so customary among the local peoples: stealing into enemy lodgings, they strike their sleeping foes on the head with these chopping knives.[4]

The natives brought us sea otters, deer hides, and fish to trade. For a large halibut I paid them a four *arshin* string [about nine feet] of large trade beads [*korol'ki*] and a five or six *vershok* string [nine to eleven inches] of glass pearls. But they would not trade their otter for our beads and fake pearls. With disdain they even refused the nankeen cotton and various iron instruments, demanding the woolen cloth they had seen in the jackets of our *promyshlenniks*. But we had none, and so we could not trade.[5]

Gentle breezes and favorable weather lasted for several days. But then one night—I do not remember the exact date— around midnight a steady wind came up, and toward dawn it increased to the level of a violent gale. The commander of the brig ordered all sails secured except for the mainsail, which was entirely reefed, and we lay to. For three days the storm raged with undiminished strength. On the fourth day, before dawn, it suddenly eased and fell quiet; but the seas continued to run exceptionally high and a fog enshrouded us completely. Soon after sunrise the fog disappeared, and then we saw the shore not more than three *versts* [about two miles] away. We threw out the sounding line: the depth was fifteen fathoms. The calm prevented us from using the sails to move away from danger, and the swell made it impossible to tow the ship with a rowboat, forcing us to drift closer and closer to shore. Finally it brought us so close that with our naked eyes we could clearly see the birds perched on the rocks.

According to our calculations, at this point we were located opposite a bay called *Kloukoty* by the natives, the southern cape of which lies at 49° and several minutes N. Latitude.[6] When the winds are light, American ships often enter this bay, but during a storm or when the waves are high such an endeavor would be accompanied by extreme peril.

It seemed to us that the loss of the ship was inevitable, and we expected death at any moment. Then, through the grace of

God, we received a northwest wind which kept us away from the shore. This wind, however, after having favored us for six hours, turned into a terrible gale that forced us to take in all sails and heave to. Afterwards, as the storm grew calm, winds blew from various directions and at diverse strengths. By using them we moved farther south.

On October 29th, sailing before a moderate south wind, we approached the coast and passed to the south of Destruction Island, which lies at 47° 33' N. Latitude. But, to our misfortune, there was no suitable anchorage and we found that we had to head out to sea again. Scarcely had we reached a point two or three miles from shore when suddenly it fell quiet, and the whole night passed without a breath of wind while the swell carried us toward the coast. On the afternoon of the 31st, at about 2:00, we drifted slowly past the island mentioned above, passing along the northern side, and approached some rocks not more than a mile from terra firma.

The commander of the brig, Navigator Bulygin, uncertain how to proceed, now called together a general council. Here we agreed to steer through the rocks, hoping to drift by them toward the shore itself. We succeeded in clearing these rocks, only to find ourselves in the midst of dangerous shoals, with some rocks visible above the water and others hidden below the surface. The commander ordered an anchor dropped, and soon another; but they did not hold the vessel, and the ship continued to drift closer to shore. The remaining two anchors were dropped, and the ship then stopped—but not for long. That evening, when it had grown dark, two of our anchor cables wore through and snapped from scraping on the rocks. Around midnight the third gave way also. Shortly thereafter a fresh breeze came up from the southwest, breaking the last of our cables.

Now we were left with no means to save the brig and ourselves except to risk heading out to sea between the rocks. The wind direction would not allow us to sail back the way we had entered; and so we set out, as they say "where the eyes look." To our astonishment, despite extreme darkness, we made our way through a passage so narrow that surely no other navigator would have dared it even in broad daylight. But we had barely managed to escape this danger when the foreyard broke. Under the circumstances we could not take in the sail to make repairs. We could only keep on until repairs might be possible.

At dawn the wind shifted directly toward the coast. We were still unable to repair the foreyard, and we had no spare. Without the foresail there was not the slightest chance of tacking against the wind and moving away from the shore, which we were approaching very rapidly. Finally, at ten o'clock on the morning of November 1st, a swell cast us into the surf and then ashore at 47° 56'N. Latitude. Thus the brig met its fate.

Now it was necessary to think about our own safety. We had to save ourselves, and also to rescue our firearms, our only means to preserve our liberty. If captured, we would live out a miserable life as slaves of the savages, a consequence a hundred times more horrible than death. The surf was pounding our ship from side to side in an awful fashion and the hold was already full of water. With weapons in our hands, we waited for the instant a large wave struck, broke against the ship, then flowed away from shore. At this moment we jumped overboard and ran for the dry land beyond the line of the surf. There we carried arms and ammunition passed to us by our companions who remained on the brig. By great good fortune it happened that we had struck on a sandbank that was soft ground and above water at low tide. Every part of the ship had been shaken loose and it was full of water; but even so it remained whole, and when the tide receded it was left on dry land.

Immediately we took the cannon, powder, and various other necessities from the ship. Next we cleaned the firearms and loaded them with fresh charges of powder, making ready to beat off an attack of the savages, who we now had cause to fear more than anything else on earth. Finally we set up two tents made from the ship's sails, which we pitched about seven *sazhens* [about fifty feet] apart. Nikolai Isaakovich [Bulygin] and I took the smaller tent for ourselves. With this much accomplished, we lighted a big fire to warm and dry ourselves.

We had hardly completed these first tasks when a large number of the natives, who had seen us land, came close. Meanwhile the navigator had taken four *promyshlenniks* with him and set out for the brig, intending to save the topmasts and sails while removing the upper rigging so the ship would roll less at high tide. As a precaution they took along a slow match, since several cannon still remained aboard the vessel. The commander directed the work himself, standing alongside the brig. He ordered me to keep watch for any movement or attack by the savages. Near our camp we posted guards and sentries at the appropriate places.

Inside our tent remained Anna Petrovna (the wife of Bulygin), the woman of a Kodiak Aleut, myself, and a pair of the local natives who had voluntarily joined us. One of these natives, a young man who called himself a *toyon* [chieftain], invited me to inspect his residence, located not far from us. At first I agreed to go with him; but my companions, suspecting treachery from the savages, would not let me go. I tried everything to convince this *toyon* of our peaceableness and to persuade him not to harm us nor try our patience. He promised friendship and declared he would attempt to bring his fellow countrymen around to the same attitude.

Meanwhile our crewmen came to me twice to report that the *Koliuzhi* [Indians] were pilfering our things.[7] I tried to persuade our people to try as best they could not to start any fights. "Stand fast, men," I said to them, "and do the best you can. Try somehow to get them out of the camp without fighting." At the same time I protested to the *toyon* about the malicious actions of his subjects, and asked him to order them to leave us in peace. Since we did not understand each other very well, our conversation was prolonged.[8]

Even while I was reasoning with him and conducting negotiations, matters came to a head. Our men began driving the savages out of the camp, and they in turn began hurling rocks. Anna Petrovna was the first to see this, and said to me: "They are throwing stones at our men." At that very moment the *promyshlenniks* opened fire on the *Koliuzhi*. I rushed out of the tent, only to be hit with a spear that wounded me in the chest. Turning, I seized a gun and ran toward the savages. I saw the one who had wounded me. He was standing near the tent, holding a spear in his left hand and a rock in his right. He threw the rock and hit me in the head, the blow striking me so hard I could not stand, and was forced to sit down on a nearby log.

But I had gotten off a shot that brought down my foe dead on the ground.

Very soon the savages fled. In this encounter they also succeeded in wounding our commander in the back with a spear and in the ear with a rock. In addition, except for the four who had been in the boat, every last person suffered injury to a greater or lesser degree from the stoning. We killed three of the enemy, one of whom they dragged away. How many we wounded I do not know. As spoils we acquired a large number of spears, raincoats, hats, and other things left at the scene of the battle.

During the night we changed the guards around the camp once. Those not on watch gathered in the tent and bewailed their sad fate.

The next morning we made a reconnaissance of the surrounding area and selected a place that we would fortify for our protection and spend the winter. But we found the coast at this point lacking in advantages for a party in our predicament. The land was covered with dense forest, which extended so near the water that large waves washed the trees.

Soon the commander gathered us all together and revealed his plans with the following words: "Gentlemen, according to the instructions given me by the chief manager of the colonies, I know that the Company ship *Kad'iak* is coming to these shores and specifically to a harbor lying not more than sixty-five [nautical] miles from the place where we are now located. Between these two points the map shows no bay, no cove, nor even a single river. Hence we should be able to reach that harbor quite easily. As you can see, we are obviously exposed here to the threat of almost certain death. The savages could very easily exterminate us, and we have no possibility of remaining here. If we leave this place immediately, they will stay to plunder the ship and divide their loot. Most likely they will not pursue us, for they will have no need to do so."

To this speech we answered in one voice: "We place ourselves in your hands."

Accordingly, each man took two guns and a pistol, and we loaded together all the boxes of cartridges, three kegs of powder, a small quantity of foodstuffs, and we set out on our way. As for the remaining weapons, we spiked the cannon and smashed the locks on the guns and pistols, then threw them into the ocean. Powder, pikes, axes, and all other iron tools were also thrown into the sea.

We began our march by crossing the river on our skiff.[9] We proceeded through the forest three [nautical] miles, then halted for the evening on account of darkness and set up our camp. The night passed very quietly, as we slept under the protection of four guards.

In the morning we emerged from the forest onto the seashore, rested, cleaned our weapons, and proceeded onwards. Early in the afternoon, between one and two o'clock, two savages caught up with our party. One was the very same *starshina* [headman or elder] who had been with us in the tent at the beginning of the recent clash. We asked what they wanted. They replied that they had come to show us the way, since we would have a very winding route if we followed along the shore, and we would meet impassable cliffs. They stated there was a path through the forest, easy and straight, which they advised us to take. But they were anxious to leave us.

I asked them to wait a little bit and see the way our firearms could perform. After drawing a small circle on the board, I fired at it with a rifle from a distance of approximately thirteen fathoms [about seventy feet], hitting the target and making a hole in the board. By this act I meant to demonstrate to them the danger they would meet if they were thinking about attacking us. The savages examined the hole in the board, measured the distance, then left us.

That night we camped in the forest at the foot of a cliff where, by chance, we discovered a cave for shelter. During the night a violent rain and snow storm struck. In the morning the wind quieted, but the miserable weather continued and forced us to spend the day in the cave. Rocks fell from the cliff near us during the day. At first we could not figure out the cause. Then we discovered that our enemy, the savages, had pushed them off the cliff to hit us. This we realized when three of these people raced past us, running along the path we had to take.

The following morning the weather turned clear and beautiful. We set out again on our route, and near midday we came

47

to a small but rather deep stream. Alongside this stream ran a well-traveled path, which we followed in the hope of finding a crossing place. Toward night we came to a single large hut. No one was there, but it held a great amount of dried coho salmon.[10] A fire was burning nearby, and in the stream alongside this hut was a weir for catching the fish. We took twenty-five dried salmon and left about three fathoms [about eighteen feet] of glass beads and several large trade beads, knowing that these articles were highly valued by the local savages. Having paid for the fish in this manner, we left the hut and went into the forest some one hundred fathoms [600 feet] and made camp for the night.

In the morning, just as we were ready to leave, we discovered that we were surrounded by a number of the savages armed with spears, harpoons, and arrows. I moved forward and, not wanting to kill or wound any of them, I fired a shot over their heads. The noise of the shot and the whistle of the bullet had the desired effect: the *Koliuzhi* scattered and ran, hiding themselves among the trees, and we were able to proceed on our way. My God! Who will believe that there might exist on the face of the earth such a cruel, barbaric people like those among whom we now found ourselves! We had left a small number of arms and abandoned our ship with all its cargo to these savages. They plundered and burned the ship and, still not satisfied, chased us down to take our lives. To them we were neither a threat nor a danger. But it seems they begrudged our very existence.

[For two days,] until November 7th, it can thus be said, we retreated from the savages, who kept on pursuing us, waiting for a good chance to launch an overwhelming attack on us. All the while they kept us under surveillance. But on the morning of this day we met three men and one woman who gave us some dried fish, and who began a tirade against that tribe from which we had just suffered while praising their own tribe. These people came along with us, and together we arrived late in the evening at the mouth of a small river.[11] On the other side was located their settlement, which consisted of six large lodges. We asked them for a boat to cross the river, but they told us to wait until full tide, saying that it was difficult to cross the river at low tide. At night, they said, when the tide was up, they would take us across. But we would not agree to go with them in the darkness and, after moving back about a *verst* [about two-thirds of a mile], we camped for the night.

Early the next morning we returned to the mouth of the river and demanded to be taken across. About two hundred savages were sitting around their lodges at the time. They answered not a word. We waited for several minutes, then started upstream to find a convenient place where we might cross. The *Koliuzhi* saw our intent and immediately sent out toward us a canoe manned by two naked boatmen. Since this canoe could carry only about ten persons, we asked for another, to make sure we could all cross at once. The savages complied with our request. They sent another canoe, but one which could carry at the most only four persons. In it was the same woman who had been with the three men we had met earlier on the trail. The persons who took seats in her boat were Mrs. Bulygin, one Kodiak island woman [Maria], the young apprentice [Filip] Kotel'nikov, and one Aleut [Yakov]. The larger canoe took nine of the most daring and alert *promyshlenniks*. All the rest remained behind on the bank.

When the larger canoe reached the middle of the river, the savages in it pulled out some plugs that were stuck in holes that had been bored on purpose in the bottom of the canoe. Then they jumped into the water and swam toward the far bank. As the current carried the canoe past the lodges, the *Koliuzhi*, who were yelling in a dreadful manner, began to throw spears and shoot arrows at our people. Fortunately a crosscurrent caught the boat and swiftly swung it over to our side of the river before it filled with water and sank. In this way, by the grace of God, our men were saved in a miraculous fashion. Every man was wounded, however, and two (Sobachnikov and Petukhov) quite seriously. Those in the smaller canoe were taken captive.

The savages assumed that the guns which had been in the canoe must be wet and out of commission. Quickly they crossed to our side, armed with spears, arrows, and two guns. We foresaw their vicious intent and hastily fortified our position as best we could. The savages drew up their forces in formation about forty *sazhens* [about ninety yards] from the position we held, then began to shoot their arrows at us and fired a single gun shot. We still had several dry guns with which we fought off the enemy, driving them away within half an hour. Before they took flight many of their warriors were wounded and two were left behind on the battlefield. On our side Sobachnikov was mortally wounded by an arrow, part of which remained in his belly. He was in no condition to travel with us. But we could not leave him as a sacrifice to the barbarians, and so we carried him.

When we had gone about a *verst* from the scene of the battle, our wounded comrade begged us to leave him behind to die in the quiet of the forest. He was suffering unbearable pain and was not far from death. He told us to leave him so we could increase our distance from the savages, who were undoubtedly sending for reinforcements and would pursue us. We said farewell to our unfortunate friend and, mourning his sad fate, we abandoned him during his last minutes of life.

After continuing on our way the rest of the day, we found at last a suitable camping place for the night in mountains covered with forest.

The danger in which we found ourselves all during that day, the fear and unceasing concern about keeping ourselves alive, had given us no time for reflection. But that night while we rested, our first thought was of the great number of savages we had encountered. We could not understand how more than two hundred persons could fit in six lodges. Later we learned that they had gathered by plan from several places to attack us. More than fifty were from those people who had attacked us when the ship was wrecked, and many were even from Cape Grenville.[12]

Our situation seemed miserable. We felt terrified and in the depths of despair. But our unhappy commander suffered more than anyone else. For he had lost his wife, whom he loved more than himself, and knew nothing of her fate at the hands of the barbarians. Bulygin was tortured grievously. One could not look at him without being moved to the greatest sympathy and tears.

On [the following three days,] the 9th, 10th, and 11th, it poured rain. Without knowing where to go, we wandered in the forest and the mountains, trying only to escape from the savages. We feared to meet these enemies in such bad weather, when our guns would be useless. Hunger completely exhausted us. We could find no mushrooms or any other wild food, and were forced to eat tree fungus, the [walrus-hide] soles of *torbasy*, intestinal and throat *kamleia*, and the gun covers made from dressed sea lion hide.[13]

Finally even these poor provisions came to an end. We then decided to return to the river, where we had seen two lodges along the bank. But the weather turned exceptionally wet and we feared to meet a large number of savages at that place. For this reason we moved away from the coast into the forest about five *versts* [about three miles], pitched the tent and spent the night.

On the 12th we had not even a speck of food. Our commander sent a detachment into the forest to gather mushrooms among the trees. Could it be possible to satisfy [the hunger of] sixteen persons by such expedients? We resolved to butcher our steadfast friend, our unfailing sentinel, our faithful dog, and the meat was shared equally by everyone.

At this hour of misfortune Bulygin gathered us together and, with tears in his eyes, said to us all: "Brothers, I have never been in such a dire predicament before, and I have almost lost my mind. No longer do I have the strength to lead you. I now commission Tarakanov to command you, and I will also obey him myself. If he is not to your liking, then by all means choose anyone you prefer from among your comrades." But everyone declared their agreement with the selection made by Nikolai Isaakovich. He then took a piece of paper and wrote in pencil a statement regarding my elevation to commander, signed it with his own hand, and after him the statement was signed by all the others who could write.

On November 13th it rained heavily, forcing us to spend the whole day at the same place. We ate the rest of the dog meat and, not having any more food, agreed the next day to attack the two lodges we had seen.

On the 14th the weather turned in our favor and the day was clear. We crept up to the lodges and surrounded them, then yelled so that anyone inside would run out; but we found there only one captive, a boy about thirteen years old. He revealed by gestures that all the people had crossed the river, frightened by signs [of our presence]. Each of us grabbed twenty-five fish in bundles and we then started back toward camp. Scarcely had we gone one *verst* from the lodge when we saw a savage running after us, crying out something we could not understand. We feared he would reveal our hiding place, so we pointed our guns at him and this forced him to keep his distance.

Along the way my comrades—with my consent—decided to stop and eat, [making their halt] in a ravine with a small creek. Meanwhile, accompanied by the *promyshlennik* Ovchinnikov and one Aleut, I climbed the nearest hill to survey the surrounding territory. Ovchinnikov was climbing in the lead. Scarcely had he reached the top of the hill when he was struck in the back with an arrow. Seeing him hit, immediately I called out to the Aleut who was following him to pull out the arrow. But just at that moment he was also hit and wounded. I turned around and saw on the hill opposite us, beyond the creek, a vast number of *Koliuzhi*. Also I caught sight of about twenty-five warriors who were running to cut off the three of us from our comrades. The arrows meanwhile were falling all around us like hail. At once I fired my gun at them, wounding one in the leg. The savages lifted the wounded man onto their shoulders and ran off, while we reached our halting place and joined our comrades. There we attended to the wounded, finding that their injuries were not serious. We stayed two days at this place to restore our strength with food and to rest the wounded.

Here we devised and approved a new plan of action. Already the time of year made it impossible for us to reach the harbor and meet the expected ship, particularly since we did not know when we would be able to cross the river. For this reason we decided to move upriver until we came to the lake out of which it flowed, or to the most suitable place on the river for fishing. Here we would fortify a place, spend the winter, and take action in the spring according to future circumstances. After reaching this decision we marched to the river and proceeded upstream without stopping. Only when we met an impassible thicket or cliff did we move away into the mountains, but then we would soon return to the riverside again. Terrible rain, falling almost without letup, greatly impeded our march. We advanced but very slowly. Fortunately, we often came upon the natives traveling in canoes on the river. Several of them, at our invitation, came to the bank and traded us fish in return for glass beads, buttons, and other trifles.

Over the next several days we advanced a rather long distance along the winding river, but only about twenty *versts* [about 13 miles] in a direct line. Suddenly we found ourselves before the very doors of two lodges. We asked [the occupants] to trade us some fish and received a very meager amount. They declared they had no more, and blamed the shortage upon the high water that had covered the fish traps through which the salmon must pass. By necessity we were forced to take strong measures, measures which our conscience completely justified. The natives had driven us to the last stage of human misery. Consequently we had every right not only to take from their countrymen by force what we needed for our lives, but also to take vengeance upon them. From our standpoint it may thus be thought that we showed a spirit of magnanimity by not wanting to inflict on them any great physical harm. Hence, in a loud, commanding tone, we ordered the people in the lodges immediately to deliver to us all the fish they had. Our demand was instantly met, and we each took a bundle [of the dried salmon] and two sealskin bags of roe. For all of this we paid the savages well, giving glass beads and metal beads; a trade that was made, as they say, to their complete satisfaction. We then persuaded them to give us two men to help carry the provisions to our first night's camp. [With this aid] we took up our march, traveled about two *versts*, and made camp for the night. To each of the savages we gave a cotton handkerchief for their work and set them free.

The next morning two *Koliuzhi* came to our camp and very boldly entered our tent. One of them was the headman of the lodge from which we had taken the fish; the other was unknown to us. They had brought a bladder full of whale oil to trade. After talking with us about this matter, the stranger asked us whether we wanted to buy back from him our woman Anna, knowing Mrs. Bulygin by this name. This astounding proposition brought cheer to us all; but Bulygin, hearing his words, was beside himself with joy. At once we began to negotiate for her return. Bulygin offered him the last greatcoat for his wife. To the coat I added my new nankeen cotton dressing gown. All our other comrades, not excluding even the Aleuts, added something: one gave his tunic, another his baggy trousers; and at last a substantial pile was accumulated. But the savage declared that to his countrymen this was too little and he demanded in addition four guns. We did not refuse him, but stated that before concluding the deal we wanted to see Anna Petrovna. The savage agreed to give us this satisfaction, and immediately left our camp.

In a short while his countrymen brought her to the farther bank of the river directly across from us. We implored them to bring her to our side. They set her in a canoe with two men and, after coming toward our shore, halted at a distance of about fifteen or twenty *sazhens* [about thirty-five or forty-five yards] and began to negotiate with us. I could not even imagine what the unhappy couple felt during this meeting. Anna Petrovna and her spouse each melted into tears, sobbed, and could scarcely talk. Looking at them, we too wept bitterly. Only the savages remained unmoved by this pathetic spectacle. She tried to calm her husband, assuring him that they kept her well and treated her humanely. The people seized with her, she said, were alive and now were staying near the mouth of the river.

After speaking with her, we began to bargain with the savages over the purchase price. We offered all the previous articles for her and added one broken musket. But they stood firm in wanting four guns. When they saw that we hesitated to meet their demand, they quickly carried her back across the river.

At that point Bulygin, again taking on the attitude of commander, ordered me to pay the savages all they demanded. I pointed out to him that we had only one good musket for each man, that we had no tools for repairing them, and that these guns were the only things that could save us. To give away such a number of muskets would be foolish; and, if we were to engage in battle again, these same muskets would be used against us. To obey his order, I insisted, would ruin us. Hence I asked him to forgive me, but concluded that I must venture to disobey him.

For his own reasons, excusable without a doubt, he had no wish to agree with my argument. By flattery and promises he tried to persuade the others to give in to his wishes. I then stated to my comrades in a strong, decisive tone that if they agreed to hand over even one musket to the *Koliuzhi*, I would no longer be their companion but would join the savages. At this everyone, to the last man, answered together that so long as we were alive we would not surrender our weapons for any possible reason. We knew this refusal would be a shock to our distraught commander. But what else could we do! A person's life and his liberty are the most precious things on earth, and we had no wish to lose them.

After this painful episode, we moved back upriver for several days. Often we saw native voyagers in their canoes, which convinced us that a settlement must be located not far up the river. We decided we wanted to reach this settlement; but on December 10th came the first heavy snowfall, and our plans were thwarted. The snow did not melt, so we could not continue our march. Now it became essential that we give attention to the best way to spend the winter and feed ourselves. With this purpose I ordered the men to clear a space alongside the river, to cut down some trees and build a cabin. Meanwhile we lived in the tents. The problem of getting food worried us most of all.

One day toward evening, while we were building our shelter, a canoe approached in which there were three persons, one of whom was a young man. We supposed that this youth, an alert lad, must be the son of some *toyon*, and we were not mistaken. In answer to our query, he said that their settlement was located very close by. We asked if they would take one of us with them to buy fish and return him to our camp. They were pleased to agree to this proposal at once and made ready to leave with extraordinary haste. No doubt they were glad to have such an excellent chance to take one of us captive so easily. Kurmachev, one of our *promyshlenniks*, was ready to go with him. When they asked him to get into their canoe with greater speed, however, we requested that they leave a hostage with us in his place. That idea they did not like at all; but, since there was no help for it, they had to comply. We kept the savage under close guard all night. The next day we freed him when they brought back Kurmachev. He arrived, however, with empty hands. The *Koliuzhi* had given him nothing and sold him nothing. Their settlement consisted of one lodge in which Kurmachev had seen six men, in addition to the three who visited us, and three women.

The savages had deceived us. For this we decided to seek satisfaction from them by other means. We placed our guests under guard, then used their boat to send to their settlement six armed men, who seized all their fish and brought it home to our camp in the evening. Then we released our captives, giving then what presents we could. Soon afterwards an old man arrived in a canoe, bringing ninety salmon that he then traded us for brass buttons.

In several days our cabin or barracks was ready and we moved into our new home. It was rectangular, with sentry boxes at the corners for the guards. Shortly thereafter the same young man, the *toyon's* son with whom we had already done business, paid another visit to us. Again we asked him to sell us some fish but received only a brusque refusal. We placed him under guard and declared we would not allow him his freedom until he secured for us the amount of fish necessary for the winter. We demanded four hundred salmon and ten bags of roe, showing the number with marks on a stick. Once he learned our demand, he sent off his companions in a hurry, though where they were going we knew not. During the following week they returned to our camp twice, and each time they spoke quietly with our captive. The second time they came, our hostage begged us to allow some canoes with his people to pass down the river. We agreed willingly, and in half an hour thirteen canoes, in which there were up to seventy persons of both sexes, passed us. Soon these people returned and supplied us with the amount of fish and roe we had demanded. Even more important, we secured from them a canoe that could carry up to six persons. Then we released the young man, our prisoner, after presenting him with a broken gun, a cloth cloak, a patterned blanket [*odeialo sittsevoe*], and a nankeen cotton shirt. Now that we had our own canoe, we sent it out frequently with armed men to catch fish for ourselves.

The *Koliuzhi* left us alone, and we—having gained this important concession—remained for a long time the sole inhabitants of our realm of land and water. There we lived quietly all winter and had plenty of food.[14]

All winter we occupied ourselves with plans for the future. I proposed a plan my comrades approved, that we build another canoe and in the spring go upriver as far as possible. Then, after abandoning the canoes, we would go into the mountains, head south, and travel to the Columbia River, along whose banks live a people not so barbaric as those we had to deal with in our present locality. This most difficult course of action we were driven to adopt only by absolute necessity. The savages, we learned, had gathered a large force at the mouth of the river, intending to do us the utmost harm if we should attempt to leave by way of the seashore. In this case, we knew, they would pursue us relentlessly.

With our plans fixed, we made ready the canoes and were only awaiting the arrival of warm days when suddenly a totally unexpected event completely upset all our calculations. Bulygin announced that he wanted to resume command and began to act like a commander with the crew. I made not the slightest objection, turned the authority over to him, and was very glad to be rid of the worry and anxiety that accompany the responsibility of leadership in so critical a situation.

On February 8, 1809, we abandoned our cabin along with a fair amount of fish, started down the river, and then halted at the place where the *Koliuzhi* had offered us a chance to buy back Mrs. Bulygin the previous year. We saw our commander's objective and were inclined to go along. His misery and the pitiful situation of his wife we understood, and we agreed that it was better to expose ourselves to danger than to drive him to despair by opposing his plan.

While we were there an old man visited us and gave us an *ishkat* [watertight basket] of stewed *kvas*.[15] He was curious to know where we were going. We told him to the mouth of the river, and then he wanted to learn where we were going from there, but this we did not know ourselves. The old man was very obliging, but for what purpose was another matter. After seeing that our fire was being drenched by a heavy downpour he left us and soon returned with two wide planks to shield it from the wind and rain. For this we gave him a handkerchief and a fur cap. He then offered to accompany us to the mouth of the river as a guide, explaining that he could protect our canoes from snags and log jams. We accepted his services and were very pleased with them. He went ahead and showed us the safest passages. Where there were many logs, he sat in our boats and guided us with great care.

In this manner we continued our journey until we came to a small island. There our guide suddenly stopped and advised us to land on the riverbank while he went across to the island, where we saw several persons rushing back and forth with bows and arrows. The old man meanwhile had pushed off, but quickly returned and told us that a large number of people had gathered on the island with the intention of throwing spears and shooting arrows at us as we passed them. He therefore proposed to take us around by another, very narrow channel, and he kept his word precisely.

When we reached the mouth of the river, we halted opposite the settlement of the savages on the other bank, where they had located their lodges and hauled their canoes out of the water onto the bank. We presented our guide with a long shirt [*rubashka*] and a neckerchief. In addition we rewarded him with a medal, stamped in this case out of pewter. On one side we depicted an eagle of sorts, which represented Russia, and on the other the year, month, and day when this savage, Liutliuliuk by name, received it. We told him to wear it around his neck.

Early the next day a large number of people came across the river to see us. Among them were two women, and one of these women was the same treacherous wench who had been party to the deception that had carried Mrs. Bulygin and the other three across the river when the savages had taken them prisoner. We immediately seized the women and one young man, tied them up, and declared to their countrymen that we would not free them until they returned our captives.

Soon the husband of one of the captive women came to us. He convinced us that our people were not there, since they had fallen by lot to another tribe, but that he would go after them and would return them all to us within four days if only we would promise not to kill his wife. Our commander, hearing this promise, was overwhelmed with joy, and we immediately decided to spend several days there.

Because the land was very low and it flooded at night when the wind was strong, we moved to a hill located about a *verst* away and fortified the place.

Eight days after our talks regarding an exchange of prisoners, about fifty *Koliuzhi* men came to the opposite bank and wanted to open negotiations with us. With several of my comrades I immediately went down to the edge of the river. The savages were commanded by an elderly man dressed in a European jacket, trousers, and a beaver hat. With them, to our great joy, we saw our Anna Petrovna.

After preliminary greetings, Mrs. Bulygin declared that the woman we held was the sister of the *toyon* who was dressed in European fashion, that both she and her brother were very fine people who had rendered her many services and had treated her very well, and she demanded that we free the woman at once. When I told her that her spouse would free the captives only on condition of an exchange for herself, Mrs. Bulygin gave us an answer that struck us like a clap of thunder, an answer we could not believe for several minutes, taking it all for a dream. In horror, distress, and anger, we heard her say firmly that she was satisfied with her condition, did not want to join us, and that she advised us to surrender ourselves to this people. The *toyon*, she explained, was an upright and virtuous man, widely known along this coast. He honestly would free us and send us to the two European ships then cruising in the Strait of Juan de Fuca.[16] Concerning the three others captured with her, she said that Kotel'nikov had been taken by a people who lived at Cape Grenville, Yakov by the people on whose shores our ship had been wrecked, and Maria by the local people there at the mouth of the river.

To Bulygin, who loved his wife passionately, I did not know what to say concerning her answer and her intentions. In vain I attempted to persuade her to come to her senses and take pity on her unhappy spouse, to whom she was indebted for everything. [But she would not change her mind.]

For a long time [after returning to our fort] I hesitated [to tell Bulygin]. Yet nothing could be done. It was impossible to hide the truth. I had to disclose everything to our anguished commander, and let him be overwhelmed.

He heard me out, but apparently did not believe me at first, assuming that I was joking. But, after reflecting a few moments, he suddenly fell into a frenzy, grabbed a gun, and ran towards the riverbank, intending to shoot his wife. After several steps, however, he stopped short and began to weep, then ordered me to go along to argue with her, and even to threaten that he would shoot her.

I carried out the instructions of my commander, but without success. His wife had decided to stay with the savages. "I do not fear death," she declared. "It is better for me to die than to wander about with you in the forest, where we might fall into the hands of a cruel and barbarous people. Now I am living with kind and humane people. Tell my husband that I scorn his threats."

Bulygin listened carefully to my report. For a long time he was silent, standing like a man who had lost his memory. At last he gave a sudden cry and fell to the ground as though dead. When he came to his senses we had laid him on a greatcoat, and he began to sob bitterly and said not a word to us.

Meanwhile, leaning back against a tree, I had time to think about the difficulty of our situation. Our commander, losing a wife who had betrayed his love and devotion and now despised him, did not understand himself what he was doing, and even wanted to die. Must we perish for that?

Following this reasoning, I posed a question to Bulygin and all our comrades: If Anna Petrovna, being a Russian, praises this people, then is it possible that she has been instructed by the savages and has agreed to deliver us into their hands? No! We must believe her. We must conclude that it would be better to entrust ourselves to them, to place ourselves voluntarily under their authority, than to wander about in the forest, continually struggling with hunger and against the elements, fighting the savages, exhausting ourselves, only to end by falling prey to some wild beast or another.

Bulygin was silent but all the others rejected my argument and would not agree with me. Then I stated that I would no longer attempt to convince them, but that for myself I had decided to act as I had proposed and voluntarily give myself up to the savages. At that moment our commander declared his opinion: he agreed with me completely. Our comrades then asked permission to reconsider. In this manner our talk ended that day. The savages headed off toward the mouth of the river and we remained on the hill to spend the night.

The next morning the savages again appeared at the former place and began anew to beg us to free our captives. At this point I announced to the *toyon* that five of our company—the navigator, Tarakanov, Ovchinnikov, and two Aleuts—considering his people honorable and virtuous, had decided to surrender to them, expecting that they would do us no harm and would allow us to depart for our homeland on the first ship to appear. The *toyon* assured us that we would not regret our decision, and he tried to persuade the others to follow our example. But they were obstinate and would not alter their course. The prisoners were released, and then our comrades bid us farewell, like brothers, with tears. We joined the savages and went with them while our comrades remained at that place.

The next day we reached the settlement of Kunishat, where the man to whom I had been allotted, the *toyon* mentioned above, Yutramaki by name, made his home that winter.[17] Bulygin was assigned to the same master, but by his own wish went to another, the one to whom his wife belonged. Ovchinnikov and the Aleuts also fell into "various hands," as the saying goes.

As for our other comrades, on the same day we parted they determined to go to Destruction Island. But during the trip they hit a rock, their canoe was smashed, all their powder got wet, and they just barely escaped with their lives. Since they had lost their only means of defense, they wanted to overtake us and surrender themselves to the Kunishat people. But they did not know the route and so ran into another tribe while they

61

were crossing a river. These savages fell on them, took them all into captivity, and later traded several to the Kunishats. The others they kept.

After we remained about a month at Kunishat, my master decided to go to his own house, located on Cape Juan de Fuca. Before setting out he bought back Bulygin, promising that he would soon buy back his wife also. She had already been forgiven by her husband and they were living together.

When we moved to the new residence, Bulygin and I lived quietly with our master. He treated us kindly and supported us well until he fell into a quarrel with Bulygin's former master. This man sent back [to Yutramaki, our master,] what he had been paid for Nikolai Isaakovich, which consisted of one little girl and two *sazhens* [fourteen feet] of cloth, and demanded the return of his captive. But Yutramaki refused to comply. Finally Bulygin declared that for love of his wife he constantly desired to join her, and begged that he be traded to his former master. His wish was fulfilled. But after this the savages repeatedly passed us from hand to hand, sometimes by selling, sometimes by exchanging us, or—because of kinship or friendship—gave us as gifts.

Nikolai Isaakovich and his Anna·Petrovna suffered the most bitter fate. At times they were together, at times separated, and they lived in continual fear that they would be parted forever. Death finally ended the misery of the unfortunate pair. Mrs. Bulygin passed away in August 1809, while living apart from her husband. When he learned of her death, he began even more to grieve, to pine away and, stricken with a case of the most severe consumption, gave up the ghost on February 14, 1810. When she died Mrs. Bulygin was in the hands of such an abominable barbarian that he did not even permit her body to be buried, but ordered it thrown into the forest.

Meanwhile I spent most of my time in captivity with my good master Yutramaki, who treated me as a friend, not as a prisoner. I tried to merit his kindness by all possible means. These people are complete children; any trifle pleases them. By taking advantage of their simplicity, I was able to make them love and even honor me. For example, I constructed a kite out of paper and, having made some string from animal tendons, launched it into the air. The kite, rising to its full height, amazed the savages. They attributed this invention to my genius and declared that the Russians could reach the sun. But nothing I did to serve my master outdid the "war rattle."[18] Happily, I was able to explain to him that the various tones of a rattle's sound could be made to signal the various movements in war, and that it would be extremely valuable when attacking an enemy or when retreating from one. This instrument, the "war rattle," put the finishing touch on my fame. Everyone was amazed at my intelligence and thought that few such geniuses could be left in Russia.

In September [1809] we left Cape Juan de Fuca and moved farther up the strait of the same name to spend the winter. There I built a small dirt-covered hut for myself and lived alone. During the fall I was busy shooting birds, and that winter I made wooden dishes for my master and for sale. For this work I forged a drawing knife and a notcher from nails with stones. The savages observed my work and were astonished. The *toyons* in a general gathering declared that a person as skillful as I must certainly be a *starshina* or *toyon*. After this I and my master were invited everywhere and entertained by all equally with their own *starshinas*. They were most astonished that Bulygin could have been our commander. He could not shoot birds in the summer nor use an axe well.

That winter the local natives suffered a great shortage of food, so great that they charged each other in trade a sea otter skin for ten dried salmon, and my master traded many sea otter skins for fish. Even so, several *starshinas* faced real hunger. The *promyshlenniks* Petukhov, Shubin, and Zuev fled to me because of their lack of food. My master fed them. Moreover, when their masters demanded that they be returned, he told them that they were living with me and that their return depended on me. The savages turned to me, and I let these men return to them only on the condition that they be fed and not abused.

In March [1810] we moved on to a summer residence where I built another earth-covered lodge more spacious than the first one, and I fortified it with gun ports on the side which faced the sea. The fame of this building spread far and wide, and *starshinas* came from great distances to look at it and wonder.

At long last, merciful God heard our prayers and delivered us. On the 6th of May [1810], early in the morning, a double-masted vessel came into view and soon approached the shore. My master, taking me with him, at once set out for the ship. This brig was a ship from the United States called the *Lydia*, under the command of Captain Brown.[19] On this ship, to my great surprise, I found my comrade Bolgusov and learned that he had been resold to someone on the Columbia River, where he had been purchased by Captain Brown. The captain, having talked with me about our misfortunes, explained to my master as best he could that he should order all his countrymen to bring to the captain all captive Russians, whom the captain would buy back. My master departed and I remained on the brig.

The next day the savages brought the Englishman, John Williams, who had been with us previously, and for whom they first asked an outrageously high ransom. Later they agreed to take five patterned blankets, five *sazhens* [about thirty-five feet] of woolen cloth, a locksmith's file, two steel knives, one mirror, five packets of gunpowder, and the same quantity of small shot. Afterwards they accepted the same quantity of goods for all of us except Bolotov and Kurmachev, whom they brought to the ship twice and both times asked such an extraordinary price that the payment for each would have exceeded the amount for all the rest of us together. When the demanded price was not paid the savages took these unfortunate people away. They also declared that we would not see Shubin either, since he had been sold to a master who had departed for Destruction Island on a whale hunt.

The stubbornness of the savages compelled Captain Brown to take other measures. He seized one of the *starshinas*, the brother of the *toyon* who held Bolotov and Kurmachev in slavery, and told him that he would not be freed until the Russians were released. This action had the desired effect. That very day they brought Bolotov and Kurmachev to us. Then we began to demand Shubin, giving them twenty-four hours [to produce him]. They brought him the following day, when we were at sea about fifteen [nautical] miles from shore. Then Captain Brown freed the chief, after paying him for each of the released people the same amount as for the others [first released].

Thus Captain Brown bought thirteen of us: Timofei Tarakanov, Dmitrii Shubin, Ivan Bolotov, Ivan Kurmachev, Afanasii Valgusov, Kas'ian Zypianov, Savva Zuev, Abram Petukhov, John Williams, two Aleut men, and two Aleut women. During our captivity seven died: Navigator Bulygin and wife, Iakov Petukhov, Koz'ma Ovchinnikov, Khariton Sobachnikov, and two Aleuts. One, the young apprentice Filip Kotel'nikov, was sold to a distant people and remained with them, and one (an Aleut) was purchased by the American captain of the ship *Mercury*, Captain [George Washington] Eayres, in 1809 on the Columbia River.[20]

On May 10th [1810] we set out on our way and sailed along the coast, often stopping at various harbors to trade with the savages; and on June 9th we arrived safely at New Arkhangel.

The crossing of the Hoh River

THE WRECK OF THE *Sv. NIKOLAI*

The Narrative of
Ben Hobucket

A Quileute Oral Tradition
The First Coming of the White People to Quileute

Transcribed by Albert S. Reagan
and published originally in
Proceedings of the
Utah Academy of Science, Arts and Letters,
Volume 6 (Provo, 1934) pp. 86-89

The Narrative of
Ben Hobucket

I n the long, long ago a ship, carrying cannon, was wrecked offshore here during a terrible storm; and, though the Indians had never seen a ship or white men before, they attempted to capture the people, but were repulsed by the cannon on the disabled ship. These people the Indians called 'ho'kwat' (wanderers) and by that name they call the white people to this day.

The ship was driven completely on the beach, and with it and a rude fortification they were able to withstand the attack of our people for a long time. For a long time they lived on 'little to eat' till all they had was eaten up. Then as they were from the Southland, they decided to try to get to their old home. So on a dark, cloudy, rainy night they stole around our village, for they had landed on the coast northwest of it; and at noon the next day they had arrived at the mouth of the Hoh River some twenty-five miles below the wreck, but they could not cross the turbulent stream.

The Hoh Indians had a village on the other side of the river, and from it Indians came over to take a look at the new people, appearing friendly. So the strangers got them to agree to ferry them across the stream. The Hohs, however, had treachery in their brains.

The white people and their belongings were placed in several canoes and the Hohs started to paddle them over; but, on reaching the middle of the stream, they suddenly opened up lightly plugged holes in the bottom of the canoes which they had intentionally cut and stuffed with cedar bark. Then, leaping from the crafts, they swam ashore, for could they get the new people adrift they could capture them single-handed without much trouble. Furthermore, they were taking them toward their own side of the river where they were prepared to attack them, should they succeed in landing. But the move did not bear the fruits expected; for, seeing that they had been duped, they quickly placed their bare feet over the holes. Then by using the breech end of their guns for paddles, they gained the river bank again near the place where the muddy, gray waters go out to meet the breakers.

Hardly had they got safe on solid ground again, however, when they were attacked by the Hohs in force, both from the river and the land side. And the Hohs had the advantage, for most of the guns were wet and the powder would not burn in them; and the cannon that had done so much execution before was at the wreck many miles away. However, the few white men who still had guns in working condition did their work well, for from behind trees they kept the enemy at bay till a fire had dried the other guns and they were brought into action. The Hohs then retreated to their own side of the river, leaving several dead on the field, besides taking several with them in their canoes. But the battle had been disastrous to the attacked as well. Three of their men, one woman and two children had been scalped [seized] and four guns had been captured. In addition, they were still on the wrong side of the river.

There was no rest for the strangers. To stay there meant attack from the enemy across the river before another sun, even if our people did not follow them and attack them in the rear. So under cover of the darkness that night they dragged themselves up the river through the underbrush, and on and on the next day they kept up their wearisome march towards the head points of the Olympics, as they are called today, till, mounting a level area among the hills, they were overcome by sheer exhaustion and fell helpless upon the moss-covered ground.

There on the following morning, weak from hunger and fatigue, they began a rude stockade. That morning a stray elk also wandered through the flat area; and a lucky shot furnished them meat, and also moccasins for their feet. And later in the day several salmon were speared in the river. So another night found them with enough to eat, roots supplying the place of bread. They, however, had no shelter from the continuous storms; and, as only one ax had been carried along with them, the preparing of anything in the form of a house or stockade was slow work. But stay here they must, for they could not ford the river; and, furthermore, before another sun had passed out of sight beyond the sparkling waters to the westward, the Hohs appeared on the opposite bank.

When the stockade and the rude bark shelters were completed, they set about to make some boats of cedar logs, using the chopping-burning process of the Indians to hollow them out, as escape by the ocean was still left to them if the fates were willing. They were not. Day after day they labored; but the Hoh Indians shut them in their stockade walls so that they could get nothing to eat but fern roots from the flat area adjacent and salmon from the immediate river. To go outside the stockade was death. Yet they could still hold out. They could still work on their boats so long as the turbulent river yielded them food; but the salmon quit running; the fishing season as we term it, came to an end. Then starvation took possession of the place. And yet the boats were not ready, for they had thought to make large boats for oar and sail. At two different times a man was then detailed to go out to kill some animal of the forest for meat and each one never came back, having fallen a victim to a Hoh arrow. Nothing was therefore left but to starve or leave the place; to be killed in the forest while looking for something to eat or to run the chances of escape by the ocean. So, though the boats were not nearly completed, an attempt at escape down the river was made.

Under the cover of clouds and darkness the unwieldy, crazy boats slipped down the river past the Indian village and had even entered the ocean when a sleepless, half-starved dog gave the alarm. And to make matters worse, an unfriendly sea met them. In an instant the ocean front was alive with savages. The unfriendly moon also appeared through a rent in the clouds and brought the fleeing people to full view. In another instant light crafts were running towards them from the shore at a terrible pace. A few shots were fired, but the boats nearest the

71

shore were overpowered and the helpless crews killed before there was time to make any resistance. Darkness, however, again closed in and the boat that was farthest out to sea escaped the fate of her sisters. Yet she was doomed.

The men labored at the oars till the blood oozed out of their fingers, but could make little progress against the heavy, rolling sea; and the women dipped water every minute to keep the boat from being engulfed. Then, as a last straw, a driving storm broke over them and drove them to the breakers.

The boat mounted a huge wave, reached its crest, paused a moment, then, as the wave broke upon a perpendicular front, it plunged forward, turned a complete somersault, bow foremost in mid-air, and disappeared in the gurgling waters. But as it was more log than boat it came to the surface again; and the struggling people climbed on to its inverted side, only to be thrown into the water by the next wave, as they had been by the previous one. Again the boat shot up to the surface, and those who still survived struggled to clamber on to it, only to be whirled over and over again in the surging waters as the next big wave pitched its crest forward. The receding waters, however, left them on solid earth again, but dazed, wet, cold, and still within the breaker line. So the next wave would surely wash over them. Creeping, crawling, stumbling, half running in the terrible darkness, they tried to gain the dry land. One of them went the wrong way and was never seen again, and several others were swept away by the undercurrent of the next wave. In fact, only five souls, four men and one woman, reached shore alive.

They landed in sight of the lights and in hearing of the Hoh head dance that had been inaugurated when the braves returned to the village with the captured dead. The contending elements had driven them back to the landing near where they had entered the ocean, on the Quileute side of the river from the village of Hoh.

At once they began to flee the certain death, or worse than death, that awaited them should daylight discover them to the frenzied Hohs, who had killed their comrades. Their guns, axes and everything had been lost. They went into the woods and started up the coast they knew not whither. Weaponless, weak from exposure, hunger and fatigue, and benumbed with cold, they pulled and dragged each other through the tangled, jungly woods.

Dawn came, but no rest. On and on they wearied themselves along until the darkness of night began to close in the eastern mountains and on and on until darkness overcame the land again. And on and on again day after day, now in this direction and now in that, hiding under logs and in the brush at the least suspicious sound, until gnawing hunger was devouring them. At last at a late hour they came in sight of the chimney blaze of the Quileute fireplaces; and hunger overcoming fear they surrendered themselves to our people.

The men were made slaves, and the woman given to one of the subchiefs for his wife; and they were forced to do the drudgery for the tribe. But as the years passed they were given more and more freedom. Then one morning after they had been here many years they were missing; and, on searching, could not be found. Some people from the Southland had made a settlement at Neah Bay and it was supposed that they had escaped thither. And the supposition was true.

Some years later a large vessel anchored in Quillayute Bay with the avowed purpose of enticing Indians on board to capture them and take them as slaves; and as many of the Quileute canoes were swarming about the apparently friendly ship with the intention of boarding her to satisfy their curiosity as to what a white man had, a woman appeared on the deck whom the Indians at once recognized as their captive.

"Go away from this place! Leave this ship! Go away! The white man's heart is not good," she hallooed to them in their own language. "If you come aboard, you will be carried away as slaves. You will never see your people again. Go away! My brothers, in the name of the God of the white man and of Kwattee and Sekahtil, your gods, I beg you to keep away from this ship." And they heeded her words and fled to the shore and to their stronghold on James Island.

The rescue off Neah Bay

THE WRECK OF THE *Sv. NIKOLAI*

Appendix:
Ivan Petrov's Fraudulent
Tarakanov Document

Appendix:
Ivan Petrov's Fraudulent
Tarakanov Document

A mong the manuscript riches of The Bancroft Library,
found in the second of seven bound volumes labeled
"Russian America," is a penciled document entitled
"Statement of My Captivity Among the Californians by a Russian Fur-Hunter." This document purports to be the account of
one Vasilii Petrovich Tarakanov, an employee of the Russian
American Company, describing his adventures during a long,
peril-filled tour of duty in California and Hawaii. Forty-two
pages long, the document is written in the hand of Ivan Petrov,
a translator, researcher, and writer for Hubert Howe Bancroft
during the 1870s. On the face of it, the document is a translation from an original narrative that Tarakanov had related to a
Russian Orthodox missionary priest at Unalaska, a certain Father Ivan Shishkin. A statement by Father Shishkin, also written
in Petrov's hand and included as part of the translation, declares
that the missionary set down this account a year after Tarakanov had returned from his adventures to his home in Unalaska.[1]

Petrov and other Bancroft assistants used this Tarakanov account when they produced Bancroft's history of Alaska and the
second volume in his history of California. Then Adele Ogden
made it a primary source in the research for her work, *The
California Sea-Otter Trade*. In 1953 the manuscript was published in full by Glen Dawson, with an introduction and notes
prepared by Arthur Woodward.[2] Since that time the account
has been cited frequently by other scholars of the Russian colonial enterprise along the Pacific Coast. Perhaps more to the

point, later authors came to depend upon the references to this document made by Bancroft, Ogden, and others, giving Petrov's manuscript a wide secondary influence.

As a survey of the literature soon indicates, the document has created a profound confusion regarding the identity of Timofei Tarakanov, giving rise to the supposition that two Tarakanovs actually appeared in about the same places at nearly the same times. As a result, the names of the two have been mixed up by a number of authors, and Vasilii has received the credit for some exploits that were undoubtedly the work of Timofei.[3]

Did Petrov create this confusion? In 1963 Professor Morgan Sherwood published an article that first suggested the need for caution in dealing with Ivan Petrov's contributions to historical knowledge. Other scholars, in particular Richard A. Pierce and Theodore C. Hinckley, soon published additional evidence regarding Petrov's remarkable career. Petrov was a man who sometimes found it convenient to invent splendid stories about his own past, and on more than one occasion he also demonstrated a loose regard for the canons of historical veracity. Sherwood and Pierce agreed that the purported journal of Father Juvenal, a Russian Orthodox monk killed by Alaskan natives in 1796, was almost certainly a fake. And in his 1968 article that best summed up a detailed investigation, Professor Pierce specifically called attention to the Vasilii Tarakanov account as another document of dubious authenticity. The supposed Vasilii Petrovich Tarakanov, Pierce then did not hesitate to state, was actually Timofei Tarakanov, and the account was false in many details.[4]

Once we began our own inquiry, we found two added facts to reinforce quite strongly these reasons for skepticism. First, the Petrov manuscript account is the only original document found anywhere that contains the name of Vasilii Tarakanov. No other primary source related to this era, whether in Russian, Spanish, or any other language, makes use of this name. Either Tarakanov is identified only by his last name in other primary documents, or he is plainly called Timofei Tarakanov. Secondly, there is no independent contemporary verification for the central story told in the Petrov manuscript, the tale of Tarakanov's capture and imprisonment with his Aleut companions for more than a year at some unnamed Franciscan mission in southern California. Although the incident, like other similar episodes, would have prompted by necessity an extensive exchange of correspondence between Franciscan missionaries, Spanish officials in California, and Russian officers, so far as these alleged events are concerned there remains a conspicuous blank in the documentary record. The Petrov manuscript remains the sole authority for this entire piece of historical narrative.

From our original doubts, an extensive search for relevant evidence now demands a conclusion that Vasilii Petrovich Tarakanov is a fictional figure, entirely the invention of Ivan Petrov. Beyond all reasonable doubt, Petrov's manuscript account of Tarakanov's narrative in The Bancroft Library is a fraud, another fabrication by Bancroft's trusted expert on Russian Alaska. As with the Juvenal journal, the Tarakanov narrative is a hoax that Petrov perpetrated upon Hubert Howe Bancroft; and as with the Juvenal journal also, this documentary fraud became a historical prank that has touched a wide community of scholars and writers interested in the record of Russia's colonial activities in North America.

One by one, the established criteria of documentary criticism sustain this conclusion. At the outset, since the manuscript in question purports to be a translation from a Russian original, can the original be produced? At the head of the manuscript, in Petrov's handwriting, is the notation "Morskoi Sbornik, November 1852." This publication, the Russian *Naval Journal*, very often printed accounts of exploration and sea-going adventure during the mid-nineteenth century. But, as Richard Pierce made certain, the original for this episode does not appear in the *Morskoi Sbornik* for November of 1852; neither can it be found in any other edition of that journal. Nothing similar to this narrative has yet come to light in any documentary collection, Russian or American. There is no reference to it within the small collection of Petrov papers at The Bancroft Library. So far as can presently be determined, the original does not exist.[5]

What about the supposed author of the original document? According to the manuscript, Father Ivan Shishkin took down this account from Vasilii Tarakanov at Unalaska soon after the fur hunter had returned, Odysseus-like, to a faithful, waiting wife. If we date from the Hawaiian and California events mentioned in the narrative, that must have been in 1819 or 1820. But the first Russian Orthodox mission at Unalaska was not authorized until 1823, and the first priest who arrived there, according to available records, was the renowned Father Veniaminov in 1824.[6] Moreover, though there was a large Shishkin family in western Siberia and Alaska during the nineteenth century, thus far no record of any Father Ivan Shishkin has been discovered. The scholar most familiar with the extensive documentary materials relating to the Russian Orthodox Church in Alaska, Professor Antoinette Shalkop, has identified 303 Russian Orthodox priests, Alaskan and Siberian, and has not found the name Ivan Shishkin. As Professor Shalkop points out in a personal communication, it may be that a Father Ivan Shishkin will come to light in records that have still to be restored and opened for examination; but to August 1980 the record remained blank.[7] We cannot authenticate the identity of the supposed author of the original document.

One physical clue in the manuscript itself provides strong circumstantial evidence of fraud. Vasilii Tarakanov claims in the narrative that he left Sitka in 1814 with a party of Aleuts aboard a ship bound for California. The manuscript contains a blank space left for the name of the ship. Had the author actually been translating from the original, of course the name would have been right there before him. Did Petrov mean to look up a reference and later fill in the appropriate ship's name? If so, he neglected this detail once the account was finished. Though a small point, it is a telling one.

The narrative is constructed upon a bare framework of historical fact, apparently derived from Russian works that Petrov had available. In particular this manuscript accords roughly with K. T. Khlebnikov's classic biography of Aleksandr Baranov, published in 1835, and P. A. Tikhmenev's standard history of the Russian American Company, originally published in two volumes between 1861 and 1863. Petrov translated large sections from both these works for Bancroft.[8] It is significant that Khlebnikov and Tikhmenev both refer to Tarakanov, but without providing the man's first name and patronymic. Hence anyone who meant to expand on these sources would have to supply, either from other sources or from imagination, the full name of this person.

That Petrov made abundant use of his imagination in writing this account is suggested by both the style and the substance of his narrative. Historical inconsistencies and exaggerations mark the document. Time and again the author attempts to make the account all too exciting. One melodramatic episode quickly follows another. Aleuts are killed off in great profusion. American ship captains and Spanish Franciscan missionaries become arch villains. The description of mission life and the supposed events of Tarakanov's imprisonment make the work a harsh piece of anti-Franciscan propaganda. Meanwhile, the narrator is made to appear something of a simpleton, understanding by his own account only a small part of the events around him and making rather naive, coyly artless judgments about the people with whom he had contact.

For episode after episode, no independent documentation can verify the substance of the narrative. After their ship sailed from New Arkhangel, the manuscript relates, Vasilii Tarakanov and his crew of Aleut sea otter hunters were subjected to outrageously cruel treatment by the American captain on whose ship they sailed. Headed south toward California, the captain forced Tarakanov and the Aleuts to hunt in the territory of the Kolosh (Tlingit) Indians. Then, when the Kolosh attacked, the captain refused to come to his hunters' rescue, letting the Kolosh kill a number of Aleuts. Later, in California waters, an Aleut was supposedly killed by the captain in a blind rage, and two others were drowned in an attempt to reach shore for water because the captain would not allow them water from supplies on board. Among the Russian American Company records for this period, admittedly sparse, there is not a shred of evidence to substantiate the account of this unfortunate voyage. Certainly it does not match the known facts about the 1814 voyage of the *Il'men* to California, the voyage that took Timofei Tarakanov to Ross Colony.[9]

Next the manuscript describes the capture of Vasilii and eleven Aleuts by the Spanish on the southern California coast, somewhere south of the Santa Barbara Channel Islands from the indications in the narrative. For more than a year these men were kept captive at a Franciscan mission, the narrative relates. During this time, it claims, a number of Aleuts converted to the Roman Catholic faith and took native wives, while the Franciscan fathers made repeated attempts to convert the faithful Vasilii, lied to him, threatened him, and tried to corrupt him in order to get him to renounce his Russian Orthodox beliefs. Among other episodes, the manuscript describes the escape of a large group of neophytes, converted California native people, from the mission. After a few days the captive Vasilii purportedly saw many of these escapees brought back after their recapture, beaten, and gruesomely tortured. Finally, the narrative declares, orders arrived that the Russian and Aleut prisoners must be sent to Monterey or San Francisco. With seven Aleut companions, Vasilii was supposedly marched to Monterey, a journey of ten days, then sent to "Mission Francisco," where he could be returned to the waiting Russian authorities.

Not one of these events can be authenticated or corroborated in the surviving contemporary documents, either Russian or Spanish. In a rough way the story of Russian and Aleut sea otter hunters being captured by the Spanish is similar to the misfortunes that overtook two small parties from the *Il'men*, one including Boris Tarasov and the other headed by John Elliot de Castro, a Portuguese in the Russian service. But the Spanish took these men prisoner in September of 1815, not in 1814 as the timing established by the Petrov manuscript would require.[10]

The surviving Spanish archives, an extensive body of governmental reports and correspondence, contain many documents that attest to these later captivities. But a careful search has not yielded one document that refers in any way to the purported capture, imprisonment, and release of Vasilii Tarakanov and his Aleut companions. The Franciscan mission records, which include a very substantial file of correspondence among various missionary priests, also fail to provide a single scrap of evidence that would authenticate the tale told in this manuscript. No document mentions Russian captives being placed at any southern California mission. There is no account of Aleut converts. No recorded rebellion of California Indian neophytes at any mission remotely matches the events in this narrative. No missionary or civil authority in Spanish California refers to the release of such a group to the Russians.[11]

But the case does not rest on negative evidence alone. At one point in the narrative there is strong positive evidence that confirms every critical suspicion. The manuscript states that Vasilii and the seven Aleuts were turned over to Lieutenant Kotzebue in San Francisco, then taken by him to the Hawaiian Islands, where they arrived after a stormy voyage of six weeks. In fact Otto von Kotzebue, a lieutenant in the Imperial Russian Navy, arrived in San Francisco in October of 1816, commanding the brig *Rurik* on a scientific expedition. At San Francisco he did take custody of three Russians and John Elliot de Castro, who were turned over to him by Governor Vicente de Sola. According to Adelbert von Chamisso, an émigré French naturalist who sailed with Kotzebue, the three Russians were old employees of the Russian American Company who had deserted but now wished to return because they missed the language and the customs of their homeland. One was named Ivan Stroganov; the other two are identified only in the Spanish records, where they are called Diego and Gregory. Kotzebue's report, Chamisso's account, and the pertinent Spanish documents make it certain that no Aleuts were taken aboard the *Rurik*.[12] On November 1st the *Rurik* sailed for the Hawaiian Islands, found a fair wind, and arrived there November 24th, with neither the delay nor the storms described in the Petrov manuscript.[13] These major discrepancies expose the manuscript as a hoax.

A significant omission in the manuscript reinforces the conclusion of fraud. Before the *Rurik* sailed from San Francisco, one of the three rescued Russians, Ivan Stroganov, was mortally wounded when his powder horn caught fire and blew up during a hunting trip ashore. His companions carried the suffering man back aboard the *Rurik*. He died there and was buried at sea. This episode, dramatic in the extreme, received mention both by Kotzebue and Chamisso in their separate descriptions of the *Rurik*'s voyage.[14] Petrov's manuscript makes no mention of Stroganov or his death; yet this incident is the very type of remarkable event that elsewhere figures so prominently in the story of the so-called Vasilii.

A further section of the narrative describes Vasilii's adventures in the Hawaiian Islands, where he purportedly became involved in that episode of comic opera imperialism that Richard Pierce has called Russia's Hawaiian adventure. The manuscript's narrative, compared with the documents that Pierce has translated and published, is wildly inaccurate. But the manuscript account contains one critical phrase: "After Sch[a]effer's flight," it reads, "I was left in charge of the settlement and the Company's property."[15]

Unmistakably this reference indentifies not Vasilii but the real Timofei Tarakanov. As we know from a number of documents, including his own signed reports, Timofei took an important role in the schemes of Dr. Georg Schaeffer, a German adventurer who had been employed temporarily by Aleksandr Baranov, to manipulate the native rulers and establish Russian sovereignty in the Hawaiian Islands. After those efforts failed, Timofei was left the leader among the Company employees when Dr. Schaeffer sailed from the Islands. He remained at Oahu with more than forty men, Russians, Creoles, and Aleuts, under his command.[16] Plainly the manuscript's author meant to appropriate the historical identity of Timofei Tarakanov at this point for his own fictional figure, the mysterious Vasilii Petrovich Tarakanov. The confusion of the two Tarakanovs had its origin in Petrov's original, deliberate hoax.

Once the confusion is explained, the gross historical inaccuracies in the Hawaiian section of the narrative give further proof of the manuscript's fraudulent character. The real Tarakanov arrived in Hawaii aboard the *Il'men* in early May 1816, not aboard the *Rurik* in November or December of that year. The *Rurik* never sailed to Kauai (Atuvai) but remained at Honolulu on Oahu until mid-December, then departed for the South Pacific. Tarakanov became established at the Russian American settlement on Kauai as far more than the laboring drudge portrayed in the Petrov manuscript. He acted as Dr. Schaeffer's most trusted subordinate and actually received his

84

own grant of land and villages from King Kaumaulii (Tamari). The manuscript makes Tarakanov say: "Sch[a]effer was a bad man who treated us all like slaves." The statement is totally unrealistic, as demonstrated best by Tarakanov's own authentic reports from the Hawaiian Islands.

When Dr. Schaeffer left Kauai, he did not abandon the Russian American Company's men. Instead he took personal command of the leaky ship *Kad'iak* and, in June 1817, sailed with Tarakanov and the other Company employees to Oahu, where they found an uncertain refuge inside the harbor at Honolulu. A month later Dr. Schaeffer left Hawaii on the ship *Panther*, headed toward St. Petersburg, apparently on the advice of Tarakanov and his companions. When Schaeffer departed, he asked or directed Tarakanov to take command and look after the Company's property as well as the other men. Altogether the documents tell an entirely different, more complex and interesting story than the simple fairy tale that appears in the Petrov manuscript.

The last pages in Petrov's literary invention are like the rest, inconsistent with historical fact. The fictional Tarakanov describes a trip back to Ross Colony in California, then tells about a last voyage that returned him finally to Alaska. The Ross Colony materials seem to be cribbed mainly from Tikhmenev's published account while the tale of the Alaskan voyage is another fantasy. The journey again is interrupted by the tyrannical demand of an American ship captain, greedy for pelts, that Vasilii and his Aleut comrades hunt for sea otter in Kolosh waters. This time, the story goes, they are forced to use some broken-down, leaky baidarkas that were being sent back from Ross Colony to Alaska. Many Aleuts, of course, lost their lives in this hazardous duty while Vasilii once more managed a narrow escape. At last, the narrative declares, Tarakanov reached Alaska and was sent back to Kodiak Island, his home, along with the only two remaining comrades from his imprisonment by the Spanish. Although they had been given up for dead, the story ends, Vasilii's wife was still waiting for him because Aleksandr Baranov had given her hope of his return.

In reality, Timofei Tarakanov came to Alaska directly from the Hawaiian Islands at the end of 1817 or early in 1818, then was despatched back to the Islands to help settle the Company's affairs with King Kamehameha and King Kaumaulii. Whether or not he actually made the trip, the documents do not show.[17]

The import of this documentary fraud, Ivan Petrov's literary hoax, deserves brief comment. It is unlikely that we shall ever know Petrov's true motives in writing this historical fantasy. Perhaps he meant to impress Mr. Bancroft with this evidence of his research initiative and translating skills. One of Petrov's contemporaries remarked that he was a lazy person; perhaps he found it easier to invent a new source than translate an old one. Perhaps he had some desire to add, in this peculiar way, his own distinctive, original influence to Bancroft's work. And perhaps the hoax was also, as we suppose, an amusement, a diversion or leisure-time occupation that he enjoyed as a sort of intellectual challenge. It may even be that he used the project to fill in idle shipboard hours during his 1878 Alaskan voyage on Bancroft's behalf. If so, Petrov supplied an entertainment not only for himself but, a century later, for others with similar historical interests.

Pacific Coast historiography has not been drastically influenced by Petrov's small venture in documentary originality, yet the consequences of his hoax were more than negligible. At one time this document did contribute to a false image of hostility between Spanish Californians, especially the Franciscan missionaries, and the Russians during the 1810s and 1820s. In its description particularly of the Franciscans' barbarous abuse and torture of native peoples, Petrov's fraud gave an appearance of historical substance to extreme anti-Franciscan prejudices. In addition, the document has lent credibility to an equally prejudiced interpretation of the relations between the Russian fur hunters and their Aleut auxiliaries or employees during this same era. It also contributed formerly to a false portrayal of the character of Dr. Georg Schaeffer and the history of Russian activities in the Hawaiian Islands.

A modern generation of scholars, utilizing a body of authentic sources that simply were not available in Bancroft's time, have discounted the prejudiced, unjust attitudes represented in Petrov's manuscript. Because the account simply does not accord with the substantial weight of evidence, it has largely been disregarded in recent studies.[18] The document has been left a sort of unexplained anomaly, a dubious source for the specialists who gave it their brief attention.

The document became important during the course of research into Timofei Tarakanov's career. Once it is dismissed as a hoax, the way is cleared for a more accurate appraisal of Tarakanov's role in Russian American history. With the record corrected, Vasilii Petrovich Tarakanov can be assigned to a place in historical fiction, his "Statement of my Captivity Among the Californians" given its proper niche in the gallery of historical frauds. No source document, the manuscript can be regarded as an amusing memorial to its author, that clever, talented storyteller Ivan Petrov, whose prolific imagination and practiced pencil duped Bancroft and many others.

THE WRECK OF THE *Sv. NIKOLAI*

Notes

Notes

Introduction

1. This summary is based on Tarakanov's inventory, which appears at the conclusion of his narrative. The term Aleut was applied by the Russians not only to the natives of the Aleutian Islands but as well to all the Alaskan Innuit peoples, including the Kaniagmiuts or Koniagas who made Kodiak Island their homeland. For further discussion see John R. Swanton, *The Indian Tribes of North America*, B.A.E. Bulletin 145 (Washington, D.C.: U.S. Government Printing Office, 1953); W. H. Oswalt, *Alaskan Eskimos* (Chicago: Chicago University Press, 1967); and Henry A. Coppock, "Interactions between Russians and Native Americans in Alaska, 1741–1840," Ph.D. diss. (Michigan State University, 1969).

2. The strategy of Russian expansion in America receives modern treatment in Nicolai N. Bolkhovitinov, *The Beginnings of Russian-American Relations, 1775–1815*, tr. Elena Levin (Cambridge, Mass.: Harvard University Press, 1975); Howard I. Kushner, *Conflict on the Northwest Coast: American-Russian Rivalry in the Pacific Northwest, 1790–1867* (Westport, Conn.: Greenwood Press, 1975); and James R. Gibson, *Imperial Russia in Frontier America: The Changing Geography of Supply of Russian America, 1784–1867* (New York: Oxford University Press, 1976). The best account of Baranov's career remains the classic biography by K. T. Khlebnikov, *Baranov: Chief Manager of the Russian Colonies in America*, tr. Colin Bearne, ed. Richard A. Pierce (Kingston, Ontario: Limestone Press, 1973).

3. Abraham Plotnikov, another survivor, gave testimony that identified among the survivors a man he called Taradanov. The similarity in names has convinced some writers that Plotnikov really meant Timofei Tarakanov. That possibility had been given wide currency by Hector Chevigny, who wove Plotnikov's few shreds of testimony into an elaborate scenario that placed Tarakanov at the center of the drama, in *Lord of Alaska: Baranov and the Russian Adventure* (New York: Viking Press, 1942). Plot-

nikov's testimony appeared in an appendix to the second volume of Petr Aleksandrovich Tikhmenev's *Istoricheskoe obozrenie obrazovaniia Rossiisko-Americanskoi kompanii i deistvii eia do nastoiashchago vremeni*, published in 1861–63 at St. Petersburg. This appendix has recently been published in English as P. A. Tikhmenev, *A History of the Russian American Company*, vol. 2, *Documents*, tr. Dmitri Krenov, and ed. Richard A. Pierce and Alton S. Donnelly (Kingston, Ontario: Limestone Press, 1979).

4. Kyrill T. Khlebnikov, *Colonial Russian America: Kyrill T. Khlebnikov's Reports, 1817–1832*, tr. Basil Dmytryshn and E. A. P. Crownhart-Vaughan (Portland: Oregon Historical Society, 1976), p. 6; Adele Ogden, *The California Sea-Otter Trade, 1784–1848* (Berkeley and Los Angeles: University of California Press, 1941), pp. 45–47

5. Richard A. Pierce, ed., *Documents on the History of the Russian-American Company*, tr. Marina Ramsay (Kingston, Ontario: Limestone Press, 1976), pp. 174, 177.

6. Khlebnikov, *Colonial Russian America*, pp. 6–7; P. A. Tikhmenev, *A History of the Russian-American Company*, tr. and ed. Richard A. Pierce and Alton S. Donnelly (Seattle: University of Washington Press, 1978), pp. 112–13; Ogden, *California Sea-Otter Trade*, pp. 50–51, 160–61.

7. Khlebnikov, *Baranov*, pp. 69–70; Tikhmenev, *History*, pp. 112–13, 131–33.

8. Richard A. Pierce, *Russia's Hawaiian Adventure, 1815–1817* (Berkeley and Los Angeles: University of California Press, 1965), pp. 9–10 and n. 14, p. 221.

9. Document 58 in Pierce, *Russia's Hawaiian Adventure*, pp. 147–52.

10. Vasilii Mihailovich Golovnin was born in April 1776 in the village of Gulyniki in Riazan' Oblast. He graduated from naval cadet school in 1792, then gained further training by service in the British navy between 1801 and 1805. He circumnavigated the globe in the sloop *Diana* in 1807–09, a feat followed by service in Russian America and the Kurile Islands. Between 1811 and 1814 he was held prisoner by the Japanese, an experience that became the subject for his earliest published work. He again circumnavigated the globe in the sloop *Kamchatka* in 1817–19. Two years later he became the assistant director of the naval cadet schools, and in 1823 he received appointment as quartermaster general of the Russian navy. Highly educated, with great talent as an administrator, he directed the navy's shipbuilding, commissariat, and artillery departments with notable success. During this same period he published a number of works based on his experiences. Golovnin rose to the rank of rear admiral. He died of cholera in St. Petersburg in 1831. His son, A. V. Golovnin (1821–1886) followed his father into a naval career; and he became a director of the journal *Morskoi Sbornik*. Through his son's efforts the writing of V. M. Golovnin were collected and published in five volumes under the general title *Sochineniia i Perevody* [*Works and*

Translations], which appeared at St. Petersburg in 1874. Biographical sketches of both men appear in the seventh volume of the *Great Soviet Encyclopedia* (New York: Macmillan, 1973), a translation of the third edition of *Bol'shaia Sovetskaia Entsiklopediia*, ed. A. M. Prokhorov (Moscow, 1970). Among other sources, a detailed account of Golovnin's career may be found in Ella Lury Wiswell, tr. and ed., *Around the World on the* Kamchatka, *1817–1819* (Honolulu: Hawaiian Historical Society and the University Press of Hawaii, 1979).

11. A biographical note on Albert B. Reagan by Vasco M. Tanner, accompanied by a bibliography of his publications, appears in *Proceedings of the Utah Academy of Sciences, Arts and Letters*, vol. sixteen (1939), pp. 5–19. For locating this item we are indebted to Director Donald K. Nelson and University Archivist Hollis Scott, Brigham Young University Library.

12. Perhaps related to this incident, a Makah tradition describes an episode when a number of Makah men were taken to California aboard the *Mercury* (Captain G. W. Eayres) and there abandoned. These men then walked back up the coast to their homeland. See Eric Blinman, Elisabeth Colson, and Robert Heizer, "A Makah Epic Journey: Oral History and Documentary Sources," *Pacific Northwest Quarterly*, 68 (October 1977), pp. 153–63.

13. John Meares, *Voyages Made in the Years 1788 and 1789, From China to the North West Coast of America* (London: Logographic Press, 1790), pp. 157–58.

14. An introduction to Quileute ethnography appears in George A. Pettitt, *The Quileute of La Push, 1775–1945* (Berkeley and Los Angeles: University of California Press, 1950).

15. Frederick William Howay, "Indian Attacks Upon Maritime Traders of the North-west Coast, 1785–1805," *Canadian Historical Review*, 6 (December 1925), pp. 287–309; and the recent scholarly summary, Warren L. Cook, *Flood Tide of Empire: Spain and the Pacific Northwest, 1543–1819* (New Haven: Yale University Press, 1973), esp. pp. 72–77 and 103–04. For the site of the *Sonora* disaster *see* Herbert K. Beals, tr. and ed., *For Honor and Country: The Diary of Bruno de Hezeta* (Portland: Western Imprints, The Press of The Oregon Historical Society, 1985), pp. 74–75, 143 n. 34.

16. An early ethnographic description may be found in James G. Swan, *The Indians of Cape Flattery, at the Entrance to the Strait of Fuca, Washington Territory* (Washington, D.C.: Government Printing Office, 1868; reprint ed., Seattle: Shorey Book Store, 1964).

17. John Rodgers Jewitt, *A Narrative of the Adventures and Sufferings of John R. Jewitt: Only Survivor of the Crew of the Ship* Boston, *During a Captivity of Nearly Three Years Among the Savages of Nootka Sound.* (Middletown, Conn.: Loomis and Richards, 1815).

18. Samuel Hill, "Autobiography," pp. 12–13, Manuscripts and Ar-

chives Division, New York Public Library. Jean R. McNiece gave valuable assistance by locating and making available a copy of this manuscript.

19. Cook, *Flood Tide*, pp. 54—79.

20. J. C. Beaglehole, ed., *The Journals of Captain James Cook on his Voyages of Discovery*, 3 vols. (Cambridge, England: The Hakluyt Society at the University Press, 1955—1969), esp. vol. 3, p. 1095.

21. Primary sources on McKay are the following: James Strange, *Journal and Narrative of the Commercial Expedition from Bombay to the Northwest Coast of America* (Madras, India: Madras Public Records Office, 1928), p. 22; J. Meares, *Voyages*, pp. 1i—1ii and 131—32; and George Dixon, *A Voyage Round the World, but More Particularly to the Northwest Coast of America* (London: Goulding, 1789), pp. 132—33. See also the summary in Cook, *Flood Tide*, pp. 100—03.

22. Cook, *Flood Tide*, pp. 234—49 and passim.

23. Tikhmenev, *History*, pp. 41—45, 61—68; Khlebnikov, *Baranov*, p. 12 ff.

24. For shipping information see F. W. Howay, *A List of Trading Vessels in the Maritime Fur Trade, 1785—1825*, ed. Richard A. Pierce (Kingston, Ontario: Limestone Press, 1973). The fur trading context is described in Ogden, *California Sea-Otter Trade*; and in Paul Chrisler Phillips and J. W. Smurr, *The Fur Trade*, 2 vols. (Norman: University of Oklahoma Press, 1961).

25. Khlebnikov, *Colonial Russian America*, p. 6; Ogden, *California Sea-Otter Trade*, pp. 50—52.

26. Khlebnikov, *Colonial Russian America*, 107; Khlebnikov, *Baranov*, pp. 70—71

27. Essential accounts of the Ross Colony enterprise include Tikhmenev, *History*, pp. 131—42; Khlebnikov, *Colonial Russian America*, pp. 106—34; and Edward Oliver Essig, "The Russian Settlement at Ross," *California Historical Society Quarterly*, 12 (September 1933), pp. 191—209. For a comprehensive bibliography see John A. Hussey, comp., *Notes Toward a Bibliography of Sources Relating to Fort Ross State Historic Park California* (Sacramento: Department of Parks and Recreation, 1979).

28. "The White Indians of Colonial America," in James Axtell, *The European and the Indian: Essays in the Ethnohistory of Colonial North America* (New York: Oxford University Press, 1981), pp. 168—206. Axtell's definition of Colonial North America, it may be remarked, includes only the Atlantic coastal areas of Anglo-American settlement and trade.

Notes
Tarakanov Narrative

1. As Golovnin explains in the original Russian edition, the rank of college councillor was the sixth rank in the table of ranks established by Peter the Great.

2. Cape Flattery, called by Tarakanov the Cape of Juan de Fuca, is the farthest northwest extension of the Olympic Peninsula, forming the southern portion of the entrance to the Strait of Juan de Fuca in modern Washington State. Here and elsewhere in his narrative, Tarakanov's latitudes correspond roughly with the modern marine charts. The dates given by Tarakanov conform to the Old Style (Julian) calendar, which remained in use in Russia until the end of the Tsarist regime.

3. The canoes of the Northwest Coast were skillfully carved of a single red cedar log. The larger seagoing canoes were often fitted with highly decorated prow and stern pieces, and some were built with plank gunwales. The dimensions of the larger canoes in common use, such as Tarakanov saw, were up to forty feet in length, with a beam of seven feet, while the smaller canoes measured ordinarily fifteen to twenty feet. The grandest of these craft, however, Tarakanov may not have observed: they measured up to seventy feet in length, and could carry as many as fifty persons on extended expeditions.

4. Tarakanov describes here the most distinctive weapon of the Northwest Coast, the whalebone war club or "slave killer," which was made by the peoples of the Nootka Sound area. These items, elaborately carved, were important badges of prestige. Hence they were widely traded and displayed with some ostentation. The firearms, iron spears, and other goods of European manufacture were, of course, the result of trade between these natives and ships from England and particularly the United States, whose trading vessels had been frequenting this coast since the voyage of the *Columbia* and the *Lady Washington* in 1787–88.

5. Their experience with British and American traders had made these people obviously very selective, choosy clients, unwilling to barter their

prime sea otter for the ordinary trade items that the Russians had in store. Tarakanov's observations demonstrate the comparative disadvantage of the Russian traders in this highly competitive market.

6. Although Golovnin, unfamiliar with this coast, declares that this cove cannot be identified, Tarakanov surely refers here to Clayoquot Sound on the west coast of Vancouver Island, a short distance south of Nootka Sound. This anchorage, visited first by captains Kendrick and Gray in 1788, had become a favored harbor and rendezvous point for American trading ships while the British and Spanish engaged in their dispute over the possession of Nootka Sound.

7. *Koliuzhi*, written by most writers as *Koloshi* or *Kolosh*, was the name originally adopted by the Russians for the Tlingit people, whose territory extends from Yakutat Bay in Alaska southward along the coast and adjacent islands to the Prince of Wales and Dall islands. But the word had acquired a broader meaning in the usage of Tarakanov and his contemporaries, becoming the common term for all native inhabitants of Northwest America excluding the Aleut and Eskimo (Innuit) peoples. Like the word *Indio* in Spanish and Indian in Anglo-American usage, *Koliuzhi* became a generic term, and so is retained in this translation to indicate Tarakanov's meaning.

8. Tarakanov's account prompts the surmise that he was able to communicate in a limited way through the lingua franca of the Northwest Coast, the so-called Chinook Jargon, a trade language based largely on the Chinook language of the lower Columbia River region; a jargon that spread as early as 1810 to as far north as coastal Alaska. Subsequent passages confirm the belief that Tarakanov could make himself understood orally, and the context suggests that the Chinook Jargon would have been the most likely common language.

9. Quillayute River.

10. Tarakanov uses the word *kizhuch*, a Russian transliteration of an Innuit native word later adopted in the scientific Latin nomenclature for the coho or silver salmon, *Onocorhynchus kisutch*. This fish, caught in abundance along the Pacific coast from northern California to Alaska, is an exceedingly important food source for the people of this region. The coho enters the coastal rivers for its spawning runs from midsummer until late fall, with a spawning season that extends from October usually until the end of December. Immense numbers of the fish were once netted, trapped, and speared by the natives, who dried and smoked their catch and stored the fish in such lodges as the Russian party here encountered. Because of its finer texture and the rich oils of its flesh, many people prefer the coho to its larger relative, the Chinook or king salmon, *Onocorhynchus tshawytscha*.

11. As the Hobucket narrative confirms, the Russians had reached the Hoh River, approximately fourteen miles from their shipwreck site just north of the Quillayute River.

12. Cape (or Point) Grenville is located some three miles south of the Quinault River, which reaches the ocean twenty-eight miles south of the Hoh River.

13. Golovnin notes that *torbasy* in Kamchatka and America are the large boots that Russian fishermen sometimes call *bakhily* or peasant's boots. To his comment it may be added that they are the type of waterproof Innuit footwear now commonly called by the Eskimo term *mukluk*. The tops are made of caribou skin, the soles of seal hide: scant nourishment for Tarakanov and his hungry companions. A *kamleia*, Golovnin notes in the Russian edition, is a garment cut like a shirt, with the body sewn from bear gut and the hood from the gullets of hair seals or sea lions. Modern readers will recognize these garments as rain parkas or anoraks, which are fashioned from the intestinal material of various mammals. The use of these articles for food is testimony to the ravenous, meat-hungry appetites of the *promyshlenniks*.

14. Golovnin's Russian edition adds this comment in a footnote: "People accustomed to bread and varied edibles may consider a diet of fish alone as starvation; but our *promyshlenniks* even in good times in their own settlements almost always live on fish, to which they add all kinds of seasonings: herbs, wild roots and shellfish."

15. Golovnin explains that an *ishkat* is a basket made of twigs or roots, woven so densely that it will hold water. The word *ishkat* is another term taken over by the Russians from the Aleut language. The angelica plant [*Angelica archangelica*] Golovnin continues, is called *kvas* root because the *promyshlenniks* make a tart drink of it similar to *kvas*. Non-Russian readers may benefit from the explanation that *kvas* is a popular Russian drink made of fermented bread and berries, mildly alcoholic, similar to spruce beer or root beer.

16. It is quite possible, we may deduce from Judge Howay's information, that the *Hamilton*, Captain Lemuel Porter, and the *Otter*, Captain Samuel Hill, were trading in the area together about this time: Howay, *List of Trading Vessels*, p. 81.

17. The identity of Yutramaki is discussed in the introduction to this volume. The location of Kunishat cannot be determined. John Swanton gives Kwe-nēt-che-chat as the Makahs' name for their own people, meaning "cape people": *Indian Tribes of North America*, p. 427. In the diary of his 1790 expedition, Manuel Quimper mentioned meeting at Neah Bay a man called "Cuney," who was "apparently the chief of another settlement." See Henry R. Wagner, tr. and ed., *Spanish Explorations in the Strait of Juan de Fuca* (1933; reprint ed. New York: AMS Press, 1971), pp. 125–26.

18. Tarakanov's description suggests some implement rather like a bosun's rattle.

19. Judge Howay's sources identify the *Lydia* as a brig built in the East Indies of teakwood, owned by the Perkins firm, which cleared Boston in

April 1809 for the Northwest Coast with T. Brown as master. Subsequently, in 1813, Dr. Georg Schaeffer bought this ship in the Hawaiian Islands for the Russian American Company and it was renamed the *Il'men*. The ship cannot be identified positively as the same brig *Lydia* that rescued Jewitt and Thompson, survivors of the *Boston*, at Nootka in 1805. Tarakanov, as the appendix notes, subsequently traveled aboard the *Il'men* to California and the Hawaiian Islands. See Howay, *List of Trading Vessels*, pp. 65, 69, 84–85, 89–90, 99–100; and Tikhmenev, *History*, pp. 122, 149–50.

20. The career of Captain G. W. Eayres (or Ayres) on the Northwest Coast and in the California trade is well documented. See Howay, *List of Trading Vessels*, pp. 69, 75, 78, 86; Hubert Howe Bancroft, *History of the Northwest Coast* (2 vols. San Francisco: A. L. Bancroft & Company, 1884), vol.1, p. 324–25; Documents on the Mercury Case, 1806–1816, Special Collections, Los Angeles Public Library; and May Fidelia Boudinot, "The Case of the 'Mercury' as Typical of Contraband Trade on the California Coast, 1790–1820" (M.A. thesis, University of California, Berkeley, 1915).

Notes
Petrov's Fraudulent Document

1. The Bancroft Library catalogs this document as item P–K 2: 2. In the original, the name of the purported author is spelled Vassili Petrovitch Tarakanoff. It is described in Dale L. Morgan and George P. Hammond, eds., *A Guide to the Manuscript Collections of The Bancroft Library*, vol. 1 (Berkeley and Los Angeles: University of California Press, 1963), p. 178. Following current Bancroft Library practice, the editors modernize the spelling as Tarakanov, a precedent also adopted here.

2. Bancroft and his assistants compounded the problem at the beginning by fusing, unwittingly, the identity of Tarakanov with that of Boris Tarasov: Hubert Howe Bancroft, *History of California*, vol. 2, *1801–1824* (San Francisco: The History Company, 1886), pp. 307–08, 310–11; and *History of Alaska* (San Francisco: A. L. Bancroft & Company, 1886), pp. 493–94. Adele Ogden corrected some of the details in Bancroft's account, but did not resolve the contradictions that stemmed from her use of the Petrov manuscript: *California Sea-Otter Trade*, pp. 50, 60–61, 161, 163, 165, 168 and 198, n. 64. The Dawson publication, issued in a limited edition of 200 copies, carries the following legend on its title page: "*Statement of My Captivity Among the Californians* By Vassili Petrovitch Tarakanoff, Written down by Ivan Shishkin, & translated from the Russian by Ivan Petroff, with Notes by Arthur Woodward. Los Angeles: Glen Dawson, 1953."

3. Cook, *Flood Tide*, pp. 499-501, attributes Timofei's role in the *Sv. Nikolai* shipwreck to Vasilii. Gibson, *Imperial Russia*, transliterates Vasilii into Basil while following the Petrov manuscript for details of the Schaeffer affair in Hawaii: pp. 147–48. Hector Chevigny, *Russian America: The Great Alaskan Venture, 1741–1867* (New York: Viking Press, 1965), correctly identified Timofei in his text, but then supplies the name Vasilii Tarakanov in his bibliography. Bolkhovitinov, *Russian-American Relations*, also refers to V. P. Tarakanov: p. 183.

4. Morgan B. Sherwood, "Ivan Petroff and the Far Northwest, *Journal of the West*, 3 (July 1963), pp. 305–15, which also appeared as chapter 4,

"The Enigmatic Ivan Petroff," in Sherwood's volume *Exploration of Alaska, 1865–1900* (New Haven: Yale University Press, 1965); Richard A. Pierce, "A Note on 'Ivan Petroff and the Far Northwest,'" *Journal of the West*, 4 (October 1964), pp. 436–39; Morgan B. Sherwood, "A Note on the Petroff Note," *Journal of the West*, 4 (October 1964), p. 440; Theodore C. and Caryl Hinckley, "Ivan Petroff's Journal of a Trip to Alaska in 1878, *Journal of the West*, 5 (January 1966), pp. 25–70; and Richard A. Pierce, "New Light on Ivan Petroff, Historian of Alaska," *Pacific Northwest Quarterly*, 59 (January 1968), pp. 1–10.

5. Pierce, "New Light," *Pacific Northwest Quarterly*, 59 (January 1968), p. 5; Alton S. Donnelly to Kenneth N. Owens, August 16, 1976, personal communication in the editor's possession; Richard A. Pierce to Alton S. Donnelly, October 2, 1976, personal communication made available by Professor Donnelly.

6. Tikhmenev, *History*, p. 189; Richard A. Pierce, ed., *The Russian Orthodox Religious Mission in America, 1794–1837*, tr. Colin Bearne (Kingston, Ontario: Limestone Press, 1978), pp. 47–48.

7. Antoinette Shalkop to Kenneth N. Owens, August 2, 1980, in the editor's possession.

8. These translations are found in volumes one and four of the seven volume Russian America collection in The Bancroft Library.

9. Khlebnikov, *Baranov*, p. 98; Tikhmenev, *History*, pp. 137–39.

10. The problem is complicated by the destruction of major bodies of archival records. The St. Petersburg archives of the Russian American Company were hauled away and burned in the 1870s, after the Company's dissolution. The Company archives from the New Arkhangel office were turned over to the United States at the sale of Alaska in 1867, and came to be deposited in the National Archives. But these records are nearly blank until the closing years of Baranov's administration. Raymond H. Fisher, *Records of the Russian-American Company, 1802, 1817–1867* (Washington, D.C.: National Archives and Records Service, General Services Administration, 1971), contains a calendar of these documents. Spanish California's original archival sources went up in flames during the San Francisco fire of 1906. Fortunately, extensive transcripts of those records were made previously under the direction of Hubert Howe Bancroft and may now be consulted at The Bancroft Library. These Bancroft transcripts contain abundant evidence regarding the capture of Boris Tarasov, John Elliot de Castro, and twenty-four Kodiak sea otter hunters in September of 1815: State Papers, vol. 19, pp. 384, 385, 387–90, 393–94; and vol. 20, p. 94; Documentos para la Historia de California, Colección del José de la Guerra y Noriega, vol. 2, p. 223. The same records also document Spanish concern over Russian deserters in 1814 and the capture of the American ship *Mercury*, Captain G. W. Eayres, as well as the negotiations for the return of Boris Slobodchikov. They document, in other words, every verifiable episode of offi-

cial relations with Russians or other foreign nationals in Spanish California during these years.

11. The most important body of documents is the Santa Barbara Mission Archives, fully described in Maynard J. Geiger, O.F.M., *Calendar of Documents in the Santa Barbara Mission Archives* (Washington, C.C.: Academy of American Franciscan History, 1947). A second important collection is the published correspondence of the mission president for this period, Father José Señán: *The Letters of José Señán, O.F.M., Mission San Buenaventura, 1796–1823*, ed. Lesley B. Simpson and tr. Paul D. Nathan (San Francisco: John Howell for the Ventura County Historical Society, 1962). The best detailed treatment of mission history is found in Fr. Zephyrin Engelhardt, *Missions and Missionaries of California*, 4 vols. (San Francisco: James H. Barry Company, 1908–15). Additional information on the California mission records, including local mission archives not examined during the research for this project, may be found in Henry Putney Beers, *Spanish and Mexican Records of the American Southwest: A Bibliographical Guide to Archive and Manuscript Sources* (Tucson: University of Arizona Press and the Tucson Corral of the Westerners, 1979), pp. 282–305.

12. The pertinent sources, together with English translations, are conveniently brought together in August C. Mahr, *The Visit of the "Rurik" to San Francisco in 1816*, Stanford University Publications University Series, History, Economics, and Political Science, vol. 2, no. 2 (Stanford: Stanford University Press, 1932). See particularly pp. 42–45, 64–69, 120–23.

13. Otto von Kotzebue, *A Voyage of Discovery into the South Sea and Beering's Straits*. 3 vols. (London: 1821; reprint ed. New York: Da Capo Press, 1967), 1, 289–92.

14. Mahr, *Visit of the Rurik*, pp. 45, 69.

15. Printed in Tarakanoff, *Statement of My Captivity*, p. 32. (The pages are not numbered in the manuscript original.)

16. Pierce, *Russia's Hawaiian Adventure*, pp. 23, 101–06, and passim. This work provides the fullest, most accurate account of Dr. Schaeffer's scheme, and prints in translation the pertinent available documents. The summary here and in the following paragraphs is based on Pierce's volume.

17. Pierce, *Russia's Hawaiian Adventure*, pp. 147–52. In all likelihood Tarakanov had returned to New Arkhangel aboard the *Il'men*. The Russian American Company correspondence in the National Archives, as Professor Pierce has very kindly pointed out, offers a few additional clues to Tarakanov's activities in 1820, when he was ordered from New Arkhangel to Okhotsk aboard the brig *Finlandia*, with instructions to proceed to the Company's main office in St. Petersburg. He received these orders so he could clear up his accounts as the Company's agent for the Hawaiian Island expedition. In addition, Professor Pierce also relates, the

index to vital statistics in the Alaska Russian Church Collection at the Library of Congress notes the birth of Aleksei Tarakanov, son of Timofei, at Sitka in February 27, 1819. This information may be compared with Petrov's tale of a wife waiting at Unalaska.

18. An exception is found in James J., Rawls' *Indians of California: The Changing Image* (Norman: Oklahoma Press, 1984), p. 38. Rawls accepts the published version of the fraudulent narrative at face value and quotes the account to demonstrate the "scenes of vicious torture and cruelty" supposedly witnessed at a California mission by the fictional Tarakanov "with suppressed horror." It is regrettable that Petrov's anti-Franciscan bias has now been given renewed validation in a modern work of scholarship.

Index

Colophon

Designed and produced by Western Imprints, The Press of the Oregon Historical Society, this volume is the eighth in the Oregon Historical Society's North Pacific Studies Series.

The text and display typefaces are both Janson. This face, often confused with Jenson and mistakenly attributed to a Dutchman, Anton Janson, in actuality was cut during the last decade of the seventeenth century by Nicholas Kis, a Hungarian who worked in Amsterdam. Janson is part of the Geralde family of typefaces, with an oblique incline in all its letters, and a strong contrast between thick and thin strokes. The curved ear of the lower case g and the rounded style of the italic *v* and *w* are earmarks of Janson.

The text was set by G&S Typesetters of Austin, Texas, and the display and map typography were set by Irish Setter of Portland. This volume was printed by McNaughton and Gunn Lithographers of Ann Arbor, Michigan, on 70lb Warren Olde Style alkaline paper, and casebound in a three-piece combination of Roxite cloth and Papan paper.

Karen Beyers, a Portland artist, provided the remarkable illustrations and maps specially drawn for inclusion in this book.